Quantitative Analysis in Operations Management

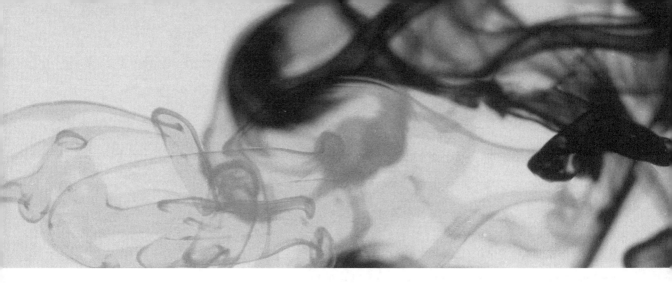

Quantitative Analysis in Operations Management

Alistair Brandon-Jones

Nigel Slack

 Prentice Hall
FINANCIAL TIMES

An imprint of **Pearson Education**

Harlow, England • London • New York • Boston • San Francisco • Toronto
Sydney • Tokyo • Singapore • Hong Kong • Seoul • Taipei • New Delhi
Cape Town • Madrid • Mexico City • Amsterdam • Munich • Paris • Milan

Pearson Education Limited
Edinburgh Gate
Harlow
Essex CM20 2JE
England

and Associated Companies throughout the world

Visit us on the World Wide Web at:
www.pearsoned.co.uk

First published 2008

ISBN 978-0-273-70848-3

British Library Cataloguing-in-Publication Data
A catalogue record for this book is available from the British Library

Library of Congress Cataloging-in-Publication Data
A catalog record for this book is available from the Library of Congress

10 9 8 7 6 5 4 3 2 1
12 11 10 09 08

Typeset in 10/12pt Sabon by 30
Printed by Ashford Colour Press Ltd., Gosport

The publisher's policy is to use paper manufactured from sustainable forests.

BRIEF CONTENTS

CONTENTS

Alistair Brandon-Jones is a lecturer in operations and supply management at Bath University and a visiting lecturer at Warwick Medical School. Previously, he was a teaching fellow at Warwick University and a visiting lecturer at the University of San Diego. Alistair holds a bachelor's degree in management science from Warwick University, a post-graduate diploma in research methodology from EIASM, Brussels, and a doctorate from Warwick University for which he received an Emerald/EFMD outstanding doctoral research award. Alistair has publications in the *International Journal of Operations & Production Management, Journal of Purchasing & Supply Management* and *Journal of Public Procurement*. He has also contributed cases, questions, and teaching notes to the last three editions of *Operations Management*. Alistair's main research interest is customer-centric service design. This work focuses on the important role that customers – either internal or external – can have in improving service delivery. His second area of research focuses on purchasing strategy. For this, he is the UK lead member for the *International Purchasing Survey* exploring purchasing practices across the world.

Nigel Slack is professor of operations management and strategy at Warwick University. Previously, he has been professor of manufacturing strategy at Brunel University, a lecturer in management studies at Oxford University, and a fellow in operations management at Templeton College. Nigel holds a bachelor's degree in engineering and a masters in management from Bradford University, a doctorate from Brunel University, and is a chartered engineer. He is the author of numerous publications in operations management, including *The Manufacturing Advantage, Making Management Decisions, Service Superiority, Cases in Operations Management, Operations Strategy, Perspectives in Operations Management, The Blackwell Encyclopedic Dictionary of Operations Management, Operations and Process Management*, and of course *Operations Management*. Nigel has also published in a wide range of academic journals, including *International Journal of Operations & Production Management, International Journal of Process Management & Benchmarking, British Journal of Management, R&D Management, International Journal of Business Performance Management, Journal of Purchasing & Supply Management* and *International Journal of Service Industry Management*. Nigel's current research interests are in operations flexibility, operations strategy, performance measurement, and the management of design and development networks.

We have really enjoyed the challenge of writing the 1st edition of this book and our thanks go to everyone who has provided input during the various stages of development. Two people in the Supply, Operations & Decision Analysis (SODA) Group at Bath School of Management deserve a special mention. Emma Brandon-Jones wrote many of the worked examples and questions throughout the book, and was actively involved in the editing process. Niraj Kumar was kind enough to develop the queuing section found in chapter two.

Our thanks also go to Eammon Ambrose of University College Dublin; Frederico Caniato of Politecnico di Milano; Mandar Dabhilkar of the Royal Institute of Technology, Stockholm; Carsten Dittrich of the University of Southern Denmark; Dirk Pieter van Donk of the University of Groningen; Donal Hughes of University College Dublin; Robert Johnston of Warwick Business School; Mike Lewis of Bath School of Management; Niall Piercy of Bath School of Management; Erik van Raaij of Rotterdam School of Management; Stefano Ronchi of Politecnico di Milano; Michael Rüdiger of the University of the Federal Armed Forces, Munich; Rhian Silvestro of Warwick Business School; and Brian Squire of Manchester Business School.

For their enduring support and encouragement, we are grateful to colleagues in the Supply, Operations & Decision Analysis (SODA) Group at Bath School of Management and in the Operations Management Group at Warwick Business School. Finally, this book could not have come to fruition without the publishing expertise of Matthew Smith, Annette Abel, Robin Stokoe and Joe Vella.

Alistair Brandon-Jones
Nigel Slack

Publisher's acknowledgements

We are grateful to the following for permission to reproduce copyright material.

Chapter 2, unnumbered table: Slack, N., Chambers, S. and Johnston, R. (2007) *Operations Management*, Fifth Edition. Harlow, England: Pearson Financial Times Prentice Hall, Table 17.6, p. 563. Reproduced by permission; Figures 4.1 and 4.2: Slack, N., Chambers, S. and Johnston, R. (2007) *Operations Management*, Fifth Edition. Harlow, England: Pearson Financial Times Prentice Hall, Figure 12.5, p. 374 and Figure 12.8, p. 378. Reproduced by permission.

In some instances we have been unable to trace the owners of copyright material, and we would appreciate any information that would enable us to do so.

Introduction

Making decisions and bearing the responsibility for them is one of the cornerstones of any operation manager's job and its importance is reflected in most texts on the subject. For example, Slack *et al.*[1] provide concepts that support decision making in four major areas: operations strategy, design, planning and control, and improvement. In common with other authors, they explore both qualitative and quantitative approaches, but the lack of space means some aspects of quantitative analysis are not fully explored or are omitted entirely. That is where *Quantitative Analysis in Operations Management* comes in.

So what do we mean by quantitative analysis? Quantitative analysis involves collecting data that can exist in a range of magnitudes and therefore can be measured in some way. Data can then be organised in such a way as to help decision making. Qualitative analysis, on the other hand, is concerned with the aspects of behaviour that indicate how and why decisions are made. The focus of most operations management texts is qualitative, and there is good reason for this. Operations management is a 'functional discipline'; it concerns the activities and decisions that are made within the operations function of an organisation. Qualitative analysis conveys the richness, the subtleties and the ambiguities that are often present in operations management decision making.

However, if we ignore quantitative techniques, we are missing the single most powerful opportunity to bring rigour and discipline to operations – decision making. Operations management is often concerned with activities, decisions and performance issues that can be expressed as numbers. 'How many customers do we need to serve?', 'How many hours should we be working this week?', 'What is our average delivery time?' and 'When will it arrive?' To make more informed decisions, it is usually beneficial to quantify different aspects of the operation. We should avoid the temptation to 'leave it to the experts', because even simple quantitative techniques enable us to estimate the consequences of decisions in a logical manner.

I.1 Models and quantification

All analysis in operations management requires that the decision is 'modelled' in some way. A model is a representation of the relevant aspects of a decision with which we are concerned. It represents a decision by structuring and formalising the information we possess and in doing so presents reality in a simplified but organised form. When we use the term model in this sense, it is

---

[1] Slack, N., Chambers, S., and Johnston, R. (2007) *Operations Management*, 5th edition. Harlow, England. Financial Times Prentice Hall.

apparent that managers communicate by means of models all the time. If a manager comes out of a meeting he or she will report back to the team not by giving a verbatim account of the meeting but by simplifying all that was discussed and condensing into a 'word picture' the meeting's main events.

Verbal descriptive models

In presenting this model of the meeting, the manager will probably be simplifying what has occurred in two ways:

(a) He or she will deliberately exclude much of what has happened and is therefore making a judgement about the relative importance of events. The manager may even reveal some of the modelling process by stating what is being excluded. For example, 'I won't bore you with the preliminaries...' or '...and there was a lot of detailed discussion until...'

(b) The manager will compress or aggregate several comments, reactions and events into one overall result. For example, the simple statement, 'They agreed to the agenda' may mean that they only did so after considerable argument but the manager judges the statement to be an adequate summary.

In this way the overall structure of the meeting will be conveyed but some of the information, richness and flavour of what occurred is inevitably lost. Also note that this 'model' of the meeting is merely descriptive. It can communicate what has happened and it can provide information on which to base a decision, but it in no way attempts to provide any kind of recommendation or answer.

Analogue models

Some models simplify reality through the use of analogy. Analogy means representing one set of properties by another. For example, a contour line on a map is an elegant method of describing the altitude of land while not interfering with other information on the map. In this way the contour map is an analogue model of the terrain it portrays. Graphs are probably the most frequently used physical (as opposed to verbal) analogue models. They represent the relationship between two variables by a line on a chart and in doing so convey the relationship between the variables in an efficient and convenient way. But the problem with analogies is that one can take them too far. Not only may there be doubts about the validity of a particular analogy, there may also be problems in projecting or extrapolating it outside the set of circumstances for which it was originally appropriate. Analogies rely on implications and associations to describe the underlying structure of a problem. A graph may indicate that, under a given set of circumstances, there is a specific relationship between, for example, quality levels achieved and a particular approach to scheduling, but it does not tell you why the relationship occurs – to do that we need to develop a relationship model.

Relationship models

A relationship model makes explicit assumptions about the links between cause and effect. The use of models that formalise the relationships between elements in a decision is a very significant step forward in the usefulness of modelling. Not only is it the most important part of understanding the problem, but the model is now capable of being translated into a more formal language such as mathematical symbols. Words, although conveying the flavour of a decision, may be ambiguous and may not focus upon the important features within the decision as effectively as a diagrammatic or mathematical formulation. Furthermore, words are essentially a serial form of modelling, that is, one idea necessarily follows another, and are therefore inadequate for complex interrelated, non-serial decision problems. By using mathematical symbols to model relationships (often called symbolic modelling), it is not only possible to convey complex relationships, it is also far easier to manipulate data in order to provide a clear guide to decision making. Table I.1 illustrates the three stages of modelling.

Table I.1 Types of decision model

Level	Types of model
Descriptive models	The 'scale of reality' is changed, e.g. a verbal summary (this table), a scale model for layout.
Analogue models	One set of properties is represented by another, e.g. graphical representations of demand, histograms etc.
Relationship models	'Influence relationships' are explicitly stated or implied. Symbolic models are relationship models where mathematical symbols, letters and numbers are used to convey the relationship between elements in the decision. Most of the techniques covered in this book fall into this category.

I.2 Why use quantitative models?

The use of quantitative models has several advantages, including the following:

- The structure of the model is transparent, so it can be easily understood and communicated.
- Transparency means that the assumptions within the model are obvious (and therefore open to challenge).
- Exploring alternative decisions using a quantitative model is simpler and faster than attempting to experiment with reality.
- Comparisons between alternative courses of action can be carried out on a more objective basis.
- Interpreting the results from a quantitative model is relatively straightforward.
- It offers at least the promise of finding the 'optimal' solution to a problem.

With the last point in mind, remember that in reality it is very unusual for a quantitative model to provide the whole answer to a real question. Whilst quantitative analysis provides a discipline and emphasis on measurable results, it is best to think of such analysis as the 'second pillar' of decision making in operations management. For a balanced approach, any manager must understand both the broad concepts that underlie operations management problems and also the quantitative techniques that enable them to be analysed.

I.3 Types of quantitative model

There are a number of dimensions upon which quantitative decision models and techniques can be classified. Here we will identify three of these dimensions, the last one of which is used to classify the various techniques described in this book.

The first dimension is to classify techniques as to whether they are trying to *optimise* or *satisfice*. Optimising techniques attempt to find the single best solution to a problem – the maximum profit or the minimum cost, for example. Satisficing techniques accept that the theoretical optimum may either be too time consuming to search for or not recognisable as the optimum even if it were found. These techniques aim for a 'good sub-optimal' solution which is likely to be better than any solution reached without the aid of the technique.

The second dimension distinguishes between *deterministic* and *probabilistic* techniques. Deterministic techniques use single estimates to represent the value of each variable in the decision, whereas probabilistic techniques use probability distributions, histograms or some other description of the range of values which a variable can take. Probabilistic models describe decisions in terms of the uncertainty inherent within them. In practice, of course, almost everything is probabilistic. In business very few things are absolutely 100 per cent certain. However, remember that modelling involves simplifying reality, which is why so many techniques adopt a deterministic approach. Those techniques that adopt a probabilistic approach can do so in two ways. Some techniques assume that certain elements of the model will take different values according to an assumed or historically derived pattern and predict an operation's behaviour, the prime determinant of which is the variability itself. Queuing models are a good example of this type. Other techniques are those which use probability to describe the decision maker's ignorance of future occurrences in a more fundamental way; here the nature of uncertainty is described much more tentatively. Decision tree models are representative of this type.

The third category, and the one we shall use in this book, classifies techniques according to *how they are used* or *what they are used for*. Using this classification, we identify four types of quantitative technique.

Predictive techniques are used to predict events occurring in the future that are largely outside the control of the manager. Using the predictions from these techniques, managers can choose an appropriate course of action. The various forecasting techniques are examples of this type.

Descriptive techniques are used for describing the reality of a decision. They often attempt to expose some underlying relationship that enables managers to make more info rmed decisions. Statistical process control is a good example of this type of technique.

Evaluative techniques focus on attempting to articulate the consequences of adopting different decision options. Usually this involves using an appropriate and standard set of criteria to compare and contrast alternative options on the same basis. Using these techniques, the manager is better able to identify appropriate courses of action. Weighted score methods are typical of this type of technique.

Optimising techniques attempt to identify the optimum (that is, the best) answer to a problem. Often these techniques involve aggregating decision criteria so that a single function representing an objective can be mathematically optimised. Linear programming is a good example of this type of technique.

CHAPTER 1

Predictive techniques

Introduction

Whilst all managers want to know exactly what is going to happen in the future, they are bound to be disappointed. However, just because the future is inherently uncertain it does not mean that predictive techniques are a waste of time and effort. On the contrary, predictive techniques can help to structure our knowledge and expectations about the future. They normally do this by developing a model that attempts to predict the probability of an outcome.

In fact almost any model which describes some aspect of the behaviour of a process or an operation, or indeed any phenomenon, can be used to predict its future behaviour. In that sense, almost all techniques and models can be said to be predictive. In this section, however, we are specifically concerned with some of the more common models or techniques which are used predominantly or exclusively for the prediction of events that are largely outside our control.

1.1 Time series analysis

Data collected at regular intervals is often called **time series data**. Examples of this might include daily sunshine, weekly production output, monthly service levels or annual demand. **Times series analysis** is a method of forecasting which examines the pattern of time series data and, by removing underlying variations with assignable causes, extrapolates future behaviour. Different types of time series methods include **moving average, weighted moving average, simple exponential smoothing, trend-adjusted exponential smoothing** and the **multiplicative seasonal model**.

Simple moving average

The **simple moving average** is used to estimate demand for a future time period by averaging the demand for the n most recent time periods. The value of n can be set at any level, but is usually in the range of 3 to 7. So, assuming n is set at 4, and the actual demand for week t is A_t, then the forecast for week t is calculated as:

$$F_t = \frac{A_{t-1} + A_{t-2} + A_{t-3} + A_{t-4}}{4}$$

WORKED EXAMPLE

Beer sales at Chico's Bar, Toronto, Canada are shown in the middle column of the following table. A 3-month (i.e. n=3) moving average appears in the right column. Using this information, we can project demand for beer in January 2009.

Month	Actual beer sales – in pints	3-month moving average
January 2008	1,625	–
February 2008	1,253	–
March 2008	1,715	–
April 2008	1,944	$\frac{1,715 + 1,253 + 1,625}{3} = 1,531$
May 2008	2,009	$\frac{1,944 + 1,715 + 1,253}{3} = 1,637$
June 2008	2,371	$\frac{2,009 + 1,944 + 1,715}{3} = 1,889$
July 2008	2,600	$\frac{2,371 + 2,009 + 1,944}{3} = 2,108$
August 2008	2,744	$\frac{2,600 + 2,371 + 2,009}{3} = 2,327$
September 2008	2,232	$\frac{2,744 + 2,600 + 2,371}{3} = 2,572$
October 2008	1,810	$\frac{2,232 + 2,744 + 2,600}{3} = 2,525$
November 2008	1,966	$\frac{1,810 + 2,232 + 2,744}{3} = 2,262$
December 2008	2,022	$\frac{1,966 + 1,810 + 2,232}{3} = 2,003$

To project demand for beer in January 2009:

$$\frac{\text{December sales} + \text{November sales} + \text{October Sales}}{\text{Sum of months}} = \frac{2,022 + 1,966 + 1,810}{3} = 1,933$$

Weighted moving average

The **weighted moving average** is also used to estimate demand for a future time period, but unlike a simple moving average each time period can be weighted to reflect its relative importance in prediction. For example, in a 3-period weighted moving average, the most recent time period may be assigned a weight of 5, the second most recent a weight of 3, and the oldest time period a weight of 2. The forecast (F) for week t is thus calculated as:

$$F_t = 5A_{t-1} + 3A_{t-2} + 2A_{t-3}$$

WORKED EXAMPLE

'The Clock and Barrel' pub decides to forecast beer
sales by weighting the past three months as follows:

Weight Applied	Period
3	Last month
2	2 months ago
1	3 months ago
6	Sum of weights

We can use the weighted moving average to project demand for beer in January 2009.

Month	Actual beer sales – in pints	3-month weighted moving average
January 2008	1,625	
February 2008	1,253	
March 2008	1,715	
April 2008	1,944	$\frac{(3 \times 1,715) + (2 \times 1,253) + (1,625)}{6} = 1,546$
May 2008	2,009	$\frac{(3 \times 1,944) + (2 \times 1,715) + (1,253)}{6} = 1,752.5$
June 2008	2,371	$\frac{(3 \times 2,009) + (2 \times 1,944) + (1,715)}{6} = 1,938.33$
July 2008	2,600	$\frac{(3 \times 2,371) + (2 \times 2,009) + (1,944)}{6} = 2,179.17$
August 2008	2,744	$\frac{(3 \times 2,600) + (2 \times 2,371) + (2,009)}{6} = 2,425.17$
September 2008	2,232	$\frac{(3 \times 2,744) + (2 \times 2,600) + (2,371)}{6} = 2,633.83$
October 2008	1,810	$\frac{(3 \times 2,232) + (2 \times 2,744) + (2,600)}{6} = 2,464$
November 2008	1,966	$\frac{(3 \times 1,810) + (2 \times 2,232) + (2,744)}{6} = 2,106.33$
December 2008	2,022	$\frac{(3 \times 1,966) + (2 \times 1,810) + (2,232)}{6} = 1,958.33$

So the demand for January 2009 is:

$$\frac{(3 \times \text{December sales}) + (2 \times \text{November sales}) + (1 \times \text{October sales})}{\text{Sum of weights}}$$

$$\frac{(3 \times 2,022) + (2 \times 1,966) + (1,810)}{6} = 1,968$$

Simple exponential smoothing

The main disadvantage of moving averages is that they do not use data from beyond n periods in forecasting. The **exponential smoothing approach** forecasts demand in the next period by taking into account the actual demand in the current time period and the forecast that was previously made. As such, the forecast takes into account past errors. It does so according to the following formula:

$$F_t = \alpha(A_{t-1}) + (1-\alpha)F_{t-1}$$

Where F_t = new forecast
A_{t-1} = previous period's actual demand
F_{t-1} = previous period's forecast demand
α = smoothing constant

WORKED EXAMPLE

In March, a computer salesman predicted April demand for 36 Iplon laptops. Actual April demand was 41. Using a smoothing constant chosen by management of $\alpha = .20$, we can forecast the May demand using the exponential smoothing model as follows:

New forecast = $F_t = \alpha (A_{t-1}) + (1 - \alpha) F_{t-1}$

$= (0.2 \times 41) + (0.8 \times 36) = 37$

Trend-adjusted exponential smoothing

The main disadvantage of simple exponential smoothing is that it assumes a stable underlying average. When there is a trend in the average, exponentially smoothed forecasts lag behind the changes in underlying demand. Whilst higher smoothing constants (>0.5) help to reduce forecast errors, there may still be a lag if the average is systematically changing. Therefore, it is possible to include a trend within exponentially smoothed forecasts to improve accuracy. The new formula is:

$$FIT_t = F_t + T_t$$

Where FIT_t = forecast including trend
F_t = exponentially smoothed forecast
T_t = exponentially smoothed trend

For a **trend-adjusted forecast**, we must smooth both the average (F_t) and the trend (T_t). The smoothing constant is shown with the β symbol for the average and the α symbol for the trend. To arrive at the forecast including trend (FIT_t), we must compute the two parts of the equation:

$$F_t = \alpha(A_{t-1}) + (1-\alpha)(F_{t-1} + T_{t-1})$$

$$T_t = \beta(F_t - F_{t-1}) + (1-\beta)T_{t-1}$$

Where F_t = exponentially smoothed forecast for period t
T_t = exponentially smoothed trend for period t
A_t = actual demand for period t
α = smoothing constant for the average
β = smoothing constant for the trend

WORKED EXAMPLE

A bank in Hong Kong uses trend-adjusted exponential smoothing to forecast demand for its mortgage applications each month. Smoothing constants are assigned values of $\alpha = 0.2$ and $\beta = 0.3$. The forecast for January was 50 applications and the trend is an increase of 5 applications each month.

Month	Actual demand (A_t)
(1) Jan	56
(2) Feb	65
(3) Mar	71
(4) Apr	?

Step 1: Forecast for February (F_2):

$F_2 = \alpha(A_1) + (1 - \alpha)(F_1 + T_1)$

$F_2 = (0.2)(56) + (1 - 0.2)(50 + 5)$

    $= 11.2 + 44$

    $= 55.2$

Step 2: Compute trend for February (T_2):

$T_2 = \beta(F_2 - F_1) + (1 - \beta) T_1$

$T_2 = (0.3)(55.2 - 50) + (1 - 0.3)(5)$

    $= 1.56 + 3.5$

    $= 5.06$

Step 3: Compute exponentially smoothed forecast including trend for February (FIT_2):

$FIT_2 = F_2 + T_2$

    $= 55.2 + 5.06$

    $= 60.26$ applications

We can now do the same calculations for March.

Step 1: Forecast for March (F_3):

$F_3 = \alpha(A_2) + (1 - \alpha)(F_2 + T_2)$

$F_3 = (0.2)(65) + (1 - 0.2)(55.2 + 5.06)$

    $= 13 + 48.21$

    $= 61.21$

Step 2: Compute trend for March (T_3):

$T_3 = \beta(F_3 - F_2) + (1 - \beta) T_2$

$T_3 = (0.3)(61.21 - 55.2) + (1 - 0.3)(5.06)$

    $= 1.8 + 3.54$

    $= 5.34$

Step 3: Compute exponentially smoothed forecast including trend for March (FIT_3):

$FIT_3 = F_3 + T_3$

    $= 61.21 + 5.34$

    $= 66.55$ applications

Finally, we can forecast demand for April.

Month	Actual demand (A_t)
(1) Jan	56
(2) Feb	65
(3) Mar	71
(4) Apr	?

Step 1: Forecast for April (F_4):

$F_4 = \alpha(A_3) + (1 - \alpha)(F_3 + T_3)$

$F_4 = (0.2)(71) + (1 - 0.2)(61.21 + 5.34)$

    $= 14.2 + 53.24$

    $= 67.44$

Worked example *continued*

Step 2: Compute trend for April (T_4):

$$T_4 = \beta(F_4 - F_3) + (1 - \beta) T_3$$

$$T_4 = (0.3)(67.44 - 61.21) + (1 - 0.3)(5.34)$$

$$= 1.87 + 3.74$$

$$= 5.61$$

Step 3: Compute exponentially smoothed forecast including trend for April (FIT_4):

$$FIT_4 = F_4 + T_4$$

$$= 67.44 + 5.61$$

$$= 73.05 \text{ applications}$$

Seasonality in forecasting

Many organisations experience seasonal patterns in their demand. For example, demand for domestic gas and electricity is higher in the winter, whilst ice cream sales are higher in the summer. Seasonal patterns are defined as regularly repeating changes in demand measured in periods of less than one year (quarters, months, weeks, days or hours). **Seasonality** is expressed in terms of how much actual values differ from the average of the time series. A popular technique for incorporating seasonality in forecasting is the **multiplicative seasonal model**, where seasonal factors are multiplied by an estimate of average demand to produce a seasonal forecast. Here, we assume that there is no trend in the data, apart from seasonality. The following steps are followed:

1 Find the average demand for each 'season' by summing the demand for that season and dividing by the number of seasons available. For example, if in March we have had sales of 80, 75 and 100 over the last three years, average March demand equals $(80 + 75 + 100) / 3 = 85$.
2 Calculate average demand over all 'seasons' by dividing total average demand by the number of seasons. For example, if total average annual demand is 1320 and there are 12 seasons (months), average demand equals $1320 / 12 = 110$.
3 Compute seasonal index by dividing average season demand (step 1) over average demand (step 2). For example, March seasonal index equals $85 / 110 = 0.77$.
4 Estimate next time period's (in this case, annual) total demand.
5 Divide this estimate by the number of seasons (in this case, 12 months) and multiply by the seasonal index to provide a seasonal forecast.

WORKED EXAMPLE

Phoenix Consulting expects to have an annual demand for 7,500 hours of supply chain strategy consulting in 2010. Using the multiplicative seasonal model, we can forecast demand for June, July and August of that year.

Worked example *continued*

Answer

Month	2007	2008	2009	Ave 07–09 demand	Ave monthly demand	Seasonal index
Jan	450	475	475	466.67	570.14	0.82
Feb	500	500	550	516.67	570.14	0.91
Mar	625	600	575	600.00	570.14	1.05
Apr	600	600	650	616.67	570.14	1.08
May	550	600	600	583.33	570.14	1.02
Jun	600	625	650	625.00	570.14	1.10
Jul	700	750	800	750.00	570.14	1.32
Aug	450	400	500	450.00	570.14	0.79
Sep	500	450	450	466.67	570.14	0.82
Oct	550	500	525	525.00	570.14	0.92
Nov	650	600	650	633.33	570.14	1.11
Dec	600	600	625	608.33	570.14	1.07
	Total average annual demand			6,841.67		

June forecast   = (7,500/12) × 1.10 = 687.50

July forecast   = (7,500/12) × 1.32 = 825.00

August forecast = (7,500/12) × 0.79 = 493.75

Trend projection

The **trend projection** technique fits a trend line to a set of historical data points and then uses this line to project future demand. A number of different trend equations can be developed (e.g. exponential and quadratic), but here we focus on a linear (straight line) trend. The **least squares method** results in a straight line that minimises the sum of squares of the vertical differences (deviations) from the line to each of the actual observations (see Figure 1.1).

The least squares line is described in terms of its y-intercept (the height at which it intercepts the y-axis) and its slope (the angle of the line) using the following equation:

$$y^> = a + bx$$

Where $y^>$ = computed value of the variable to be predicted (the *dependent variable*)

       a = y-axis intercept

       b = slope of the regression line (i.e. rate of change in y for given changes in x)

       x = the independent variable (in this case time)

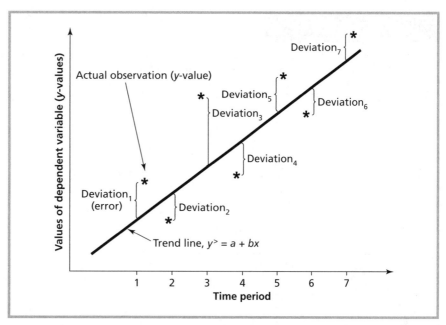

Figure 1.1 The least squares method of finding the best-fitting straight line, where the asterisks are the locations of the seven actual observations or data points

Source: Heizer, J. and Render, B. (2006) *Operations Management*, Eighth Edition. Upper Saddle River, NJ: Pearson, Figure 4.4. p. 120.

We can also find the values of a and b for any regression line using the following equations:

$$b = \frac{\sum xy - n\bar{x}\bar{y}}{\sum x^2 - n(\bar{x}^2)}$$

and

$$a = \bar{y} - b\bar{x}$$

Where x = known values of the independent variables

y = known values of the dependent variables

$\bar{x}$ = average of x values

$\bar{y}$ = average of the y values

n = number of data points

WORKED EXAMPLE

Valox Removals is trying to forecast demand for removals jobs based on historical data from 2003–8. Using the following data, we can predict demand for 2009.

Year	Demand
2003	50
2004	67
2005	74
2006	80
2007	79
2008	95

Firstly, we can calculate $\bar{x}$, $\bar{y}$, b, a, and $y^>$.

Year	Time period (x)	Demand (y)	x^2	xy
2003	1	50	1	50
2004	2	67	4	134
2005	3	74	9	222
2006	4	80	16	320
2007	5	79	25	395
2008	6	95	36	570
	$\Sigma x = 21$	$\Sigma y = 445$	$\Sigma x^2 = 91$	$\Sigma xy = 1{,}691$

$$\bar{x} = \frac{\sum x}{n} = \frac{21}{6} = 3.5$$

$$\bar{y} = \frac{\sum y}{n} = \frac{445}{6} = 74.17$$

$$b = \frac{\sum xy - n\bar{x}\bar{y}}{\sum x^2 - n(\bar{x}^2)} = \frac{1691 - (6)(3.5)(74.17)}{91 - (6)(3.5^2)} = \frac{133.43}{17.50} = 7.63$$

$$a = \bar{y} - b\bar{x} = 74.17 - (7.63 \times 3.50) = 47.47$$

Therefore, the least squares trend equation is:

$$y^> = a + bx$$

$$y^> = 47.47 + 7.63x$$

Therefore, demand for 2009 (period 7) is forecast as:

$$y^{2009} = 47.47 + (7.63 \times 7) = 100.88$$

Questions

1.1.1 Weekly sales of croissants at 'Perfect Pastries' are shown in the table below. Forecast week 7 using a 3-week moving average.

Week	Sales
1	36
2	38
3	42
4	46
5	54
6	46

1.1.2 If week 7 croissant sales are actually 38, what is the forecast for week 8?

1.1.3 If the manager assigns the following weights (most recent 0.6; second most recent 0.2; least recent 0.2) to the three months, what would the forecast for week 8 be?

1.1.4 What is the forecast for July using a 3-month moving average?

Jan	Feb	Mar	Apr	May	Jun
102	113	145	124	110	113

1.1.5 If July's actual demand turns out to be 132 and management decide to adopt a 5-month moving average, what would the forecast for August be?

1.1.6 Given the following data, calculate the 3-year moving averages for years 4 to 8.

Year	Demand
1	58
2	76
3	87
4	91
5	98
6	113
7	167

1.1.7 Recalculate the 3-year moving averages, assuming a weighting of 0.6 for the most recent year, 0.3 for the second most recent year and 0.1 for the least recent year.

1.1.8 If year 8 demand is 145, what is the weighted moving average for year 9?

1.1.9 What would the year 9 forecast be if the weightings were changed from (0.6; 0.3; 0.1) to (0.7; 0.2; 0.1)?

1.1.10 Given an actual demand of 267 flower bouquets in period 1, a previous forecast value of 250 and an alpha of 0.3, what is the exponentially smoothed forecast for period 2?

1.1.11 What would the forecast be if the smoothing constant were 0.4 instead of 0.3?

1.1.12 A salesman predicts he will sell 38 cars in March. In fact, he only sells 25. Given a smoothing constant of 0.2, what is the exponentially smoothed forecast for April?

1.1.13 In April, the car salesman sells 30 cars. What is the exponential smoothing forecast for May?

1.1.14 A customer services manager is using exponential smoothing to predict the number of calls she is likely to receive in December. The forecast for November was 4,670 calls and the actual number of calls was 4,075. Using a smoothing constant of 0.25, what is the forecast for December?

1.1.15 What is the forecast for December if the smoothing constant is changed to 0.4?

1.1.16 Use exponential smoothing with $\alpha = 0.3$ to calculate smoothed averages for birthday card sales between January and June and a forecast for July from the data below. Assume the forecast for the initial period is 76 cards.

Period	Demand
Jan	105
Feb	85
Mar	80
Apr	103
May	126
Jun	145

1.1.17 A legal firm wants to forecast demand for legal advice for period 5 based on trend-adjusted exponential smoothing. The forecast for period 1 was 74 hours, with a trend of 4 hours. The smoothing constant for the average is $\alpha = 0.3$ and for the trend is $\beta = 0.4$. For periods 2–5, complete the table below with forecasts, trends and forecast including trends.

Period	Actual (A)	Forecast (F)	Trend (T)	FIT
1	76	74.00	4.00	-
2	82			
3	83			
4	85			
5	?			

1.1.18 The legal firm decides to adjust the smoothing constant for the average to $\alpha = 0.5$ and for the trend to $\beta = 0.5$. For periods 2–5, recalculate the forecasts, trends and forecast including trends.

1.1.19 A hospital in Uganda wants to forecast demand for eye tests in year 2 using trend-adjusted exponential smoothing. The forecast demand for eye tests in the current year (period 1) was 680 tests with an annual increasing trend of 50 tests. In fact, there were 720 tests required in year 1. The smoothing constant for the average is $\alpha = 0.3$ and for the trend is $\beta = 0.2$. How many tests should the hospital plan for in year 2?

1.1.20 Demand for eye tests in year 2 is well above the forecast at 830. Calculate the trend-adjusted exponentially smoothed forecast for year 3.

1.1.21 Ice Cream Sundaze expects an annual demand for 600 tubs of mint choc chip ice cream in 2009. Using the multiplicative seasonal model, complete the following table.

Month	2006	2007	2008	Ave 06–08 demand	Ave monthly demand	Seasonal index	Forecast demand
Jan	10.00	10.00	15.00				
Feb	15.00	12.00	15.00				
Mar	15.00	20.00	17.00				
Apr	20.00	18.00	25.00				
May	50.00	45.00	46.00				
Jun	75.00	80.00	75.00				
Jul	85.00	80.00	75.00				
Aug	110.00	100.00	95.00				
Sep	75.00	70.00	85.00				
Oct	40.00	40.00	45.00				
Nov	20.00	20.00	15.00				
Dec	30.00	25.00	30.00				
Total average annual demand							

1.1.22 T.H. Harris, a home improvement supplier, is trying to predict likely demand for drills in 2009. The annual forecast is for 7500 drills. Using the multiplicative seasonal model, complete the following table and forecast demand for February, August and September.

Month	2006	2007	2008	Ave 06–08 demand	Ave monthly demand	Seasonal index	Forecast demand
Jan	300.00	250.00	275.00				
Feb	200.00	250.00	225.00				
Mar	500.00	550.00	600.00				
Apr	750.00	700.00	600.00				
May	600.00	500.00	450.00				
Jun	900.00	850.00	800.00				
Jul	1,100.00	900.00	1,200.00				
Aug	950.00	900.00	800.00				
Sep	600.00	550.00	625.00				
Oct	300.00	300.00	350.00				
Nov	250.00	225.00	250.00				
Dec	400.00	450.00	500.00				
Total average annual demand							

1.1.23 A time series trend equation is $256 + 6.7x$. What is forecast demand for period 8?

1.1.24 Broughton's Inc. in Arizona is trying to predict demand for Photographic Annual Review magazine using data for the last 6 years. Work out the least squares trend equation and forecast demand for 2009 (period 7).

Year	Demand
2003	500
2004	650
2005	700
2006	725
2007	810
2008	820

1.1.25 What is forecast demand for 2012 using the least squares trend equation?

1.1.26 Mange Tout is an outdoor catering company for large-scale functions in northern France. Using the data below, work out the least squares trend equation and forecast demand for staff in 2015.

Period	Demand
2003	56
2004	67
2005	80
2006	87
2007	80
2008	98

1.1.27 In 2009, Mange Tout actually employs 120 staff to meet demand. Recalculate the least squares trend equation and forecast demand for staff in 2015.

1.2 Associative forecasting

A limitation of time-series forecasting is that it only uses values for the forecasted variable. In contrast, **associative forecasting models** (a.k.a. **causal modelling**) can consider several variables (independent variables) that relate to the forecasted variable (the dependent variable). This section examines the most popular associative forecasting model – **linear regression analysis**.

Linear regression analysis

When applying **linear regression analysis,** we can use the same mathematical model as used in the least squares method of trend projection. The dependent variable we want to forecast is still $y^>$, but the independent variable, x, is not necessarily time. We use the following equation:

$$y^> = a + bx$$

Where $y^>$ = computed value of the variable to be predicted (the *dependent variable*)

a = y-axis intercept

b = slope of the regression line

x = the independent variable

We can also find the values of a and b for any regression line using the following equations:

$$b = \frac{\sum xy - n\bar{x}\bar{y}}{\sum x^2 - n\left(\bar{x}^2\right)}$$

And

$$a = \bar{y} - b\bar{x}$$

Where x = known values of the independent variables
y = known values of the dependent variables
$\bar{x}$ = average of x values
$\bar{y}$ = average of y values
n = number of data points

WORKED EXAMPLE

Ice Cream SunDaze wants to predict demand for choc ices based on historical data averages.

Temperature	Demand
22	500
23	600
25	750
28	800
28	850
30	910

We can see that there is clearly a linear relationship between temperature and demand for choc ices. As the temperature rises, so do sales. We can find the mathematical equation by using the least squares regression approach.

Worked example: Ice Cream SunDaze

Independent (x)	Dependent (y)	x^2	xy
22	500	484	11,000
23	600	529	13,800
25	750	625	18,750
28	800	784	22,400
28	850	784	23,800
30	910	900	27,300
$\Sigma x = 156$	$\Sigma y = 4,410$	$\Sigma x^2 = 4,106$	$\Sigma xy = 117,050$

▶

Worked example *continued*

Using the equations, we can then calculate $\bar{x}, \bar{y}, b, a,$ and $y^>$

$$\bar{x} = \frac{\sum x}{n} = \frac{156}{6} = 26.00$$

$$\bar{y} = \frac{\sum y}{n} = \frac{4{,}410}{6} = 735$$

$$b = \frac{\sum xy - n\bar{x}\bar{y}}{\sum x^2 - n(\bar{x}^2)}$$

$$= \frac{117{,}050 - (6)(26)(735)}{4{,}106 - (6)(26^2)} = \frac{2390}{50} = 47.80$$

$$a = \bar{y} - b\bar{x} = 735 - (47.80 \times 26) = -507.80$$

Therefore, the least squares trend equation is:
$$y^> = a + bx = 507.8 + 47.8x$$

We are therefore able to predict likely demand if the temperature is going to be 31 degrees centigrade.

$$y^{31\ degrees} = -507.8 + (47.8 \times 31) = 974.0$$

Questions

1.2.1 Eye-tech Inc., a pharmacy company, has identified a positive relationship between sales of eye medication (x in millions of €s) and the number of 'all clears' during eye tests (y in hundreds of thousands) by a regression equation of $y^> = 11.68 + 0.85x$. What is the forecast number of 'all clears' if sales are €33 million?

1.2.2 What if sales of eye medication increase to €45 million?

1.2.3 Karl Weber Ski School, based in Australia, have found that increases in marketing spend (€000s) have a positive impact on sales (€000s). Using the least squares regression approach, forecast demand if marketing spend is set at €90,000.

Marketing spend (€000s)	Sales (€000s)
30	203
35	225
50	334
56	350
60	413
75	551

1.2.4 The Karl Weber Ski School has also identified a relationship between the average number of ski instructors on the slopes and the number of accidents across the skiing season. How many accidents would you forecast if Karl invested in 35 ski instructors for the 2009 season?

Ski Instructors	Accidents
15	145
20	130
22	120
25	100
26	105
30	90

1.2.5   Harpal Singh is considering increasing the training budget for an e-procurement system to $120 per person. Given the data below, what level of system compliance could she expect as a result of this increase?

Training budget per person ($)	System compliance (%)
75	44
85	51
80	54
75	50
90	60

1.3   Forecast error

Having examined a number of different approaches to forecasting, we must now consider how managers decide which technique to use. The most common approach is to assess how close forecast values are to actual values. The forecast error for time period t (E_t) is calculated as actual value (A_t) minus forecast value (F_t).

MAD, MSE and MAPE

Forecast error measures the difference between forecast and actual behaviour in single time periods. However, managers are generally interested in measuring error over longer periods. The most popular methods for monitoring forecasts over multiple periods are **mean absolute deviation (MAD), mean squared error (MSE)** and **mean absolute percent error (MAPE)**.

$$MAD = \frac{\sum |E_t|}{n}$$

$$MSE = \frac{\sum E_t^2}{n}$$

$$MAPE = \frac{\sum [[E_t / A_t] 100]}{n}$$

Where n = number of forecast periods

WORKED EXAMPLE

The following table shows the forecast and actual sales of wedding albums in a photographic firm based in Tokyo, Japan. We can calculate the MAD, MSE and MAPE as follows.

(t)	Actual sales (A_t)	Forecast (F_t)	Absolute error (E_t)	Error^2 (E_t^2)	Absolute percent error
1	2,500	2,250	250	62,500	10.00
2	2,600	2,200	400	160,000	15.38
3	2,580	2,900	320	102,400	12.40
4	2,700	3,000	300	90,000	11.11
5	2,250	3,100	850	722,500	37.78
6	2,600	2,450	150	22,500	5.77

$$MAD = \frac{\sum|F_t|}{n} = \frac{2,270}{6} = 378.33$$

$$MSE = \frac{\sum E_t^2}{n} = \frac{1,159,900}{6} = 193,316.67$$

$$MAPE = \frac{\sum[[E_t / A_t]100]}{n} = \frac{92.45}{6} = 15.41$$

Questions

1.3.1   Given that forecast errors for the last four periods are −3, 6, 9, and −6, what is the mean absolute deviation?

1.3.2   A Thai restaurant based in Singapore has produced a forecast over the last 5 months. What is the mean absolute deviation (*MAD*)?

Month	Actual sales	Forecast
1	400	375
2	390	400
3	410	425
4	420	425
5	450	475

1.3.3   A Kuwaiti legal firm has forecasted demand for its partners over the last six months. What are the mean absolute deviation and mean squared error?

Month	Actual sales	Forecast
1	38	48
2	46	50
3	52	56
4	45	60
5	40	51
6	47	47

1.3.4   The following table shows the forecast and actual demand for an undertaker located in Budapest, Hungary. Calculate the *MAD*, *MSE* and *MAPE* scores for the data.

Month	Actual sales (A_t)	Forecast (F_t)
1	18	15
2	24	20
3	22	23
4	27	25
5	32	29

1.3.5   A card shop uses a smoothed forecast ($\alpha = 0.3$) to arrive at expected demand over 6 months. Calculate *MAD*, *MSE* and *MAPE* scores.

Month	Actual sales	Forecast
Jan	105	76.00
Feb	85	84.70
Mar	80	84.79
Apr	103	83.35
May	126	89.25
Jun	145	100.27

1.3.6   The card shop is considering changing their smoothing constant to 0.5.

(a) Calculate the new forecast scores.

(b) Calculate *MAD*, *MSE* and *MAPE*.

(c) Is this a better forecast?

CHAPTER 2

Descriptive techniques

Introduction

Descriptive techniques are used to represent aspects of an operation in such a way as to increase our understanding of what is being observed. Descriptive models do not seek to make causal inferences between elements in a decision; they seek to uncover and expose phenomena and to represent them in a way that will aid decision making. Descriptive techniques simplify reality, but they attempt to retain the significant elements of the decision they are dealing with. So descriptive techniques are not particularly ambitious; they do not try to give any kind of answer, they only present the facts and leave the decision to operations managers. Many managers prefer techniques that are prescriptive (that is, they give them an answer) but descriptive models are often extremely useful in finding out exactly what is happening within an operation and in aiding a more intuitive decision process.

For our purposes we can divide descriptive models into two broad categories:

- techniques that measure something
- techniques that describe behaviour.

The purpose of some descriptive techniques is simply to measure what is happening within an operation. This is not always as straightforward as it seems. Measuring capacity, for example, can be relatively complex, especially when the special circumstances connected with the mix of products or services; assumptions regarding staffing levels or predictability of equipment availability are taken into account. Many of these types of 'measuring' techniques are valuable because they provide us with a standard set of assumptions or conditions that underpin the measurement. So, for example, productivity measurement techniques provide us with a common basis for measuring productivity. It is not that the absolute measure of productivity is itself definitive. What is important is that the technique uses a transparent and standard set of assumptions that provides some standardisation to the measurement task. Other descriptive techniques describe behaviour in operations. Although we are used to thinking of the word 'behaviour' as applying only to human beings, it can also be used to describe the relationships that define process or operations behaviour. An ideal example of this type of technique is Little's Law. This simply states that throughput is equal to work in progress multiplied by cycle time. It is descriptive because it tells us exactly what will happen to one factor when one or both of the other two are changed.

2.1 Earnings before interest and tax (EBIT) and net present value (NPV)

Earnings before interest and tax (EBIT)

Marketing and product/service development play an important role in any organisation. However, it is the third core function – operations – that usually has the biggest impact on net present value profits. Sales revenue usually has to increase dramatically to have a significant effect on the bottom line of a firm. This is mainly because there are costs associated with additional sales. In contrast, any reduction in operating costs tends to have a significant effect on the profitability of the company.

WORKED EXAMPLE

Acorn Photographic currently sells 4,000 portraits each year for an average price of £60. Fixed operating costs are £80,000, whilst variable operating costs (associated with each portrait) are currently £30. John O'Reilly, the company's director, has ambitious plans to double earnings before interest and tax (EBIT) from £40,000 to £80,000 over the next year. We can explore which of the three options outlined below appears to be the most practical:

Option 1: Increase sales by 66.7% to 6,667 portraits each year through a large marketing campaign. This will increase fixed costs by £40,000.

Option 2: Start offering deluxe portraits packages and so increase the average price of portraits by 33.3% from £60 to £80. Fixed costs will remain the same, but variable costs associated with each portrait will rise from £30 to £40.

Option 3: Reduce operating costs by 33.3% by eliminating waste in the firm's operations.

Clearly, increasing sales by such a large amount will be very challenging, especially if the market is quite limited to begin with. Increasing the average price for each portrait is appealing, but one would need to consider the elasticity of demand for this service and the nature of local competition. Reducing operating costs requires no additional investment and may be the best solution in this case.

	Current	Option 1: Increase sales by 66%	Option 2: Increase price by 33.3%	Option 3: Reduce costs by 33.3%
Sales revenue	240,000	400,000	320,000	240,000
Fixed costs	–80,000	–120,000	–80,000	–80,000
Variable costs	–120,000	–200,000	–160,000	–80,000
EBIT*	40,000	80,000	80,000	80,000

*EBIT – earnings before interest and tax = net sales – operating costs.

Net present value (NPV)

When considering investments, we have to consider the time value of money. Simply put, receiving $100 today is better than receiving $100 in a year's time. We can also consider how much we would have to invest now to receive $100 in the future. This amount is called the **net present value** of receiving $100 in a year's time. For example, if the current interest rate is 5% per annum, the amount we would have to invest in now to receive $100 in one year – the net present value – is:

$$100 \times \frac{1}{1.05} = \$95.24$$

and for two years is:

$$100 \times \frac{1}{1.05} \times \frac{1}{1.05} = \$100 \times \frac{1}{(1.05)^2} = \$90.70$$

The rate of interest (5% in this case) is called the discount rate. So, we can calculate the present value (P) in n years, at a discount rate of r percent, as:

$$P = \frac{F}{[1+(r/100)]^n}$$

where F is the future value.

When the number of years is small, this equation is perfectly effective. However, when n is larger, the formula is cumbersome. For example, for 15 years, we would have to compute $(1+r/100)^{15}$. Interest rate tables, as shown below, alleviate this problem and allow us to restate the equation as:

$$P = FX$$

where F is the future value and X is the factor from the table below based on a given interest rate.

The table below shows the NPV for €1 to be paid in the future at different interest rates:

Years	3%	4%	5%	6%	7%	8%	9%	10%	12%	14%
1	€0.970	€0.962	€0.952	€0.943	€0.935	€0.926	€0.918	€0.909	€0.893	€0.877
2	€0.942	€0.925	€0.907	€0.890	€0.873	€0.857	€0.842	€0.827	€0.797	€0.769
3	€0.915	€0.889	€0.864	€0.840	€0.816	€0.794	€0.772	€0.751	€0.712	€0.675
4	€0.888	€0.855	€0.823	€0.792	€0.763	€0.735	€0.708	€0.683	€0.636	€0.592
5	€0.862	€0.822	€0.784	€0.747	€0.713	€0.681	€0.650	€0.621	€0.567	€0.519
6	€0.837	€0.790	€0.746	€0.705	€0.666	€0.630	€0.596	€0.565	€0.507	€0.456
7	€0.813	€0.760	€0.711	€0.665	€0.623	€0.584	€0.547	€0.513	€0.452	€0.400
8	€0.789	€0.731	€0.677	€0.627	€0.582	€0.540	€0.502	€0.467	€0.404	€0.351
9	€0.766	€0.703	€0.645	€0.592	€0.544	€0.500	€0.460	€0.424	€0.361	€0.308
10	€0.744	€0.676	€0.614	€0.558	€0.508	€0.463	€0.422	€0.386	€0.322	€0.270
15	€0.642	€0.555	€0.481	€0.417	€0.362	€0.315	€0.275	€0.239	€0.183	€0.140
20	€0.554	€0.456	€0.377	€0.312	€0.258	€0.215	€0.179	€0.149	€0.104	€0.073

WORKED EXAMPLE

The NPV of an investment that will pay £120 in 4 years' time, assuming a discount rate of 5%, is:

$P = FX = 120 \times 0.823 = £98.76$

Annuity values

There are circumstances when we are not trying to assess the present value of a single cash amount in the future, but a series of equal cash amounts for a number of years. The type of investment is termed an **annuity**. Whilst we could use the standard NPV equation multiple times to calculate a series of equal cash amounts, it is simpler to refer to an annuity table, like the one shown below:

Present value of an annuity of €1.00

Years	5%	6%	7%	8%	9%	10%	12%	14%
1	.952	9.43	.935	.926	.917	.909	.893	.877
2	1.859	1.833	1.808	1.783	1.759	1.736	1.690	1.647
3	2.723	2.673	2.624	2.577	2.531	2.487	2.402	2.322
4	3.546	3.465	3.387	3.312	3.240	3.170	3.037	2.914
5	4.329	4.212	4.100	3.993	3.890	3.791	3.605	3.433
6	5.076	4.917	4.766	4.623	4.486	4.355	4.111	3.889
7	5.786	5.582	5.389	5.206	5.033	4.868	4.564	4.288
8	6.463	6.210	5.971	5.747	5.535	5.335	4.968	4.639
9	7.108	6.802	6.515	6.247	5.985	5.759	5.328	4.946
10	7.722	7.360	7.024	6.710	6.418	6.145	5.650	5.216
15	10.380	9.712	9.108	8.559	8.060	7.606	6.811	6.142
20	12.462	11.470	10.594	9.818	9.128	8.514	7.469	6.623

The equation is thus:

$$S = RX$$

where S is the present value of a series of uniform amounts; R is the amount to be received annually for the duration of the investment; and X is the factor from the annuity table based on a given interest rate.

WORKED EXAMPLE

Assuming an interest rate of 8%, we can calculate the net present value of a 7-year investment which will generate €345,000 per year as follows:

$S = RX = €345,000 \times 5.206 = €1,796,070$

Questions

2.1.1   La Patisserie, a small chain of pastry outlets in Belgium, has total operating costs of €435,000. Having invested in a radio campaign, the company's sales have increased from €615,000 to €805,000. In addition to the one-off cost of €80,000 for the radio adverts, these extra sales have added €63,000 in variable costs. Thus, the total operating costs for the firm now stand at €578,000.

By what percentage has EBIT improved as a result of the marketing campaign?

2.1.2   Marie Leclerc, the CEO of La Patisserie, wants to see a similar increase in EBIT for the coming year. She is considering whether to invest in another batch of radio advertising or to try to reduce operating costs. The cost of a new radio campaign is €110,000 and she expects the same percentage increase in sales as her last campaign. If the sales growth is as forecast, Marie expects variable costs to increase by €90,000. Given that the current sales are €805,000, what do you expect the new EBIT to be if Marie goes ahead with the radio campaign?

2.1.3 Marie also has the option of not investing in the second radio campaign, but instead spending €60,000 on automated bread machines in a number of outlets. This will increase total operating costs for the year from €578,000 to €638,000. However, once up and running, it is expected that total operating costs will fall by around 30%. Sales revenue would remain at €805,000. Should Marie go ahead with the second radio campaign or invest in the automated bread machines?

2.1.4 Assuming a discount rate of 9%, what is the net present value of an investment that will pay out $30,000 in 6 years' time?

2.1.5 Assuming a discount rate of 5%, what is the net present value of an investment that will pay out £250,000 in 15 years' time?

2.1.6 Assuming an interest rate of 5%, what is the net present value of a 9-year investment that will generate $40,000 per year?

2.1.7 Assuming an interest rate of 14%, what is the net present value of a 5-year investment that will generate $55,000 per year, when the initial cost of investment is $130,000?

2.1.8 Delta Synthetics has asked you to weigh up the costs of two machines for dyeing fabric. Using the following cost information, apply the net present value method to determine which machine is the lowest total cost.

	Machine A (£)	Machine B (£)
Original cost	35,000	42,000
Labour cost p/a	5,000	7,000
Floor space p/a	1,000	1,800
Energy p/a	2,500	2,300
Maintenance p/a	4,200	1,500
Total annual cost	12,700	12,600
Scrap value	3,000	4,900
Life of machine	4 years	4 years
Discount rate	12%	12%

2.1.9 A sports centre in Riyadh, Saudi Arabia is considering investing in a new exclusive fitness suite. The net cash flows for the suite are as follows:

Year 0: −£680,000 (initial investment)
Year 1: £235,000
Year 2: £290,000
Year 3: £290,000
Year 4: £250,000

Assuming a discount rate of 7%, use the net present value table to assess whether the initial investment will be covered by year 5.

2.1.10 What if the sports centre worked using a discount rate of 14% and initial costs were actually £850,000?

2.1.11 A Swedish translation company based in Stockholm is considering new software to check translated documents for errors automatically. There is no initial investment for the software, but a fixed annual subscription of €4,000 and a variable cost of €5 per document, both paid at the end of the period. The translation company charges an average of €80 per document assessed. It forecasts demand for 400 documents in year 1, 500 in year 2 and 600 from year 3 onwards. Given a discount rate of 4%, what is the net present value of software over 4 years?

2.2 Productivity and efficiency

All operations have an interest in keeping their costs as low as possible, while maintaining appropriate levels of quality, speed, dependability and flexibility. **Productivity** and **efficiency** are two popular measures used to assess how well the operation is achieving this objective.

Productivity

Productivity is used to indicate how good an operation is at converting inputs to outputs efficiently. It is calculated as the ratio of outputs (goods and services) produced by an operation to what is required to produce them.

$$\text{Productivity} = \frac{\textit{Output from the operation}}{\textit{Input to the operation}}$$

To enable easy comparison between different operations, we can use single-factor productivity which involves dividing the output from the operation by a single input to the operation.

$$\text{Single-factor productivity} = \frac{\textit{Output from the operation}}{\textit{One input to the operation}}$$

For example, for labour productivity, the single input to the operation would be employee hours. A broader view of productivity is multi-factor productivity which includes all inputs into the operation. When calculating multi-factor productivity, all inputs must be converted into a common unit of measure, typically cost.

$$\text{Multi-factor productivity} = \frac{\textit{Output from the operation}}{\textit{All inputs to the operation}}$$

WORKED EXAMPLE

A Canadian printing firm has 15 employees and processes 725 re-print orders per week. All employees work 8 hours per day, 5 days per week. Each week, the firm spends £3,600 on wages, £1,400 on materials and £750 on overheads. Orders have an average value of £15. We can use this information to calculate single-factor labour productivity and its multifactor productivity as follows:

$$\text{Single-factor productivity} = \frac{725}{(15 \text{ employees})(40 \text{ hours per employee})} = 1.21 \text{ orders per hour}$$

$$\text{Multi-factor productivity} = \frac{725}{£3,600 + £1,400 + £750} = \frac{725}{£5,750} = 0.13 \text{ orders per pound}$$

Throughput efficiency

Throughput efficiency is a measure of the difference between processing time and work content. When the processing time of a product or service is longer than its work content, it means there are periods when no useful work is being done to materials, information, or customers who are progressing through the process. The bigger the difference, the lower the level of throughput efficiency is.

WORKED EXAMPLE

The Zucchero mail-order clothing company in Milan receives order forms; types in the customer details; checks the information provided from the customers and that the products are in stock; confirms payment and processes the order. During an average eight-hour day, 150 orders are processed. Generally, 225 orders are waiting to be processed or 'in progress'. It takes 20 minutes for all activities required to process an order. Therefore, we can calculate the throughput efficiency of the process.

Number processed = 150 orders

Time processing = 8 hours

$$\text{Cycle time} = \frac{Process\ time}{Number\ processed} = \frac{8\ hours}{150} = \frac{480\ min}{150} = 3.2\ min$$

From Little's Law, we know that Throughput Time = WIP × cycle time

Throughput time = 225 × 3.2 = 720 minutes

$$\text{Throughput efficiency} = \frac{Work\ content}{Throughput\ time} = \frac{20}{720} = 0.027 = 2.7\%$$

Despite the fact that the process is achieving a throughput time of 12 hours (720 minutes), the orders are only worked on for 2.7% of the time that they are with the company!

Value-added throughput efficiency

The approach to throughput efficiency calculation described above assumes that all the work content is actually needed. However, in many cases, there are tasks that are not actually adding value. **Value-added throughput efficiency (VATE)** limits the concept of work content to tasks that add value to the product or service. This often eliminates activities such as movement, delays and some inspections.

WORKED EXAMPLE

The Topz mail-order toy company in California receives order forms; types in the customer details; checks the information provided from the customers and that the products are in stock; confirms payment and processes the order. During an average seven-hour day, 220 orders are processed. Generally, 370 orders are waiting to be processed or 'in progress'. It takes 22 minutes for all activities required to process an order. If only 15 minutes of each order processed actually adds value, then we can calculate the value-added throughput efficiency as follows:

$$\text{Cycle time} = \frac{Process\ time}{Number\ processed} = \frac{7\ hours}{220} = \frac{420\ min}{220} = 1.9\ min$$

From Little's Law, we know that throughput time = WIP × cycle time

Worked example *continued*

Throughput time = 370 × 1.9 = 703 minutes

Throughput efficiency $= \dfrac{Work\ content}{Throughput\ time} = \dfrac{22}{703} = 0.031 = 3.1\%$

If only 15 minutes of the work content adds value then:

VATE $= \dfrac{Value\text{-}added\ work\ content}{Throughput\ time} = \dfrac{15}{703} = 0.021 = 2.1\%$

Questions

2.2.1 Quintana employees work a total of 550 hours each week producing 8,750 scarves. In an average week, 350 scarves are flawed and are sold as 'seconds' for $5, while the remaining 8,400 retail for $25. What is labour productivity per hour in terms of order and sales value?

2.2.2 The accounts department at Equinox Inc. has 5 employees, each working 7 hours per day, with overheads of £300 per day and wages of £350 per day. The team currently processes 450 invoices every day. Equinox recently invested in an e-invoice system, so now just 2 employees are required with wages of £175 per day. However, overheads now stand at £500 per day to cover the investment.

(a) What is the labour productivity (invoices per labour hour) of the old and new systems?
(b) What is the percentage change in labour productivity?
(c) What is the multi-factor productivity (invoices per pound) of the old and new systems?
(d) What is the percentage change in multi-factor productivity?

2.2.3 Qinushi sells packaged sushi to local convenience stores in Japan. The firm purchases 1,400 kilos of raw fish and, using its current equipment, produces 12 sushi meals per kilo. The firm has 100 workers averaging 6 hours per day at a total cost of 700,000 yen including overheads. Ming Sung, the production manager is considering investing in new equipment which should reduce waste and so increase production to 16 sushi meals per kilo, but pushes the total cost per day to 1,200,000 yen.

(a) What is the current labour productivity (meals per hour)?
(b) What will the impact on labour productivity be (meals per hour) if the equipment is purchased?
(c) What is the multi-factor productivity (meals per yen) of the current system?
(d) What would the new multi-factor productivity be?
(e) What would you advise Ming to do?

2.2.4 A mail order company in Moscow receives orders; types in the customer details, checks the information provided from the customers and that the products are in stock; confirms payment and processes the order. During an average eight-hour day, 480 orders are processed. Generally, 200 orders are waiting to be processed or 'in progress'. It takes 15 minutes for all activities required to process an order. What is the throughput efficiency of the process?

2.2.5 What if the number of orders processed in a day increases to 960 and the time taken for all activities falls to 10 minutes?

2.2.6 What is VATE if, of the 10-minute processing time in question **2.2.5**, only 7 minutes is value adding?

2.2.7 What is the throughput efficiency and VATE if the work content of a process is 30 minutes, the value-added work content is 20 minutes, and throughput is 90 minutes?

2.2.8 What is the throughput time and throughput efficiency if work content of a process is 50 minutes, 300 orders are in progress and in an average 6-hour day 100 orders are processed?

2.3 Capacity and requirements calculation

In order to make decisions about how best to meet demand, operations managers must first be able to measure existing capacity capabilities accurately. They can then estimate their capacity requirements for individual machines/servers or for multiple machines/servers. Finally, once requirements are known, it is possible to identify gaps by comparing requirements to available capacity, and evaluate alternatives for filling capacity gaps.

Measuring capacity

When an operation is highly standardised and repetitive, it is possible to measure capacity based on **output**. However, in many cases, operations are not standardised. In these cases, capacity is hard to measure because the output is quite ambiguous. Therefore, operations managers may look to measure capacity in terms of **inputs**.

WORKED EXAMPLE

A computer factory in Japan produces three different types of server – 400 terabyte, 200 terabyte and 100 terabyte. The 400 terabyte drive can be assembled in 2 hours, the 200 terabyte in 1.5 hours and the 100 terabyte in 1 hour. There are 650 staff hours of assembly time available each week. If demand for the 400, 300 and 100 terabyte servers is in a ratio of 3:4:2, the time needed to assemble 3 + 4 + 2 units is:

$(3 \times 2) + (4 \times 1.5) + (2 \times 1) = 6 + 6 + 2 = 14$ hours

The number of units that can be produced per week is:

$\frac{650}{14} \times 9 = 417.9$ units

Design capacity, effective capacity, utilisation and efficiency

The capacity of a process as it is designed to operate is called its **design capacity** and **utilisation** is the ratio of actual output for a process to its design capacity. In reality, it is rarely possible to achieve this theoretical level of capacity of an operation. The actual capacity of a process, once maintenance, changeover, other stoppages and loading have been considered, is termed **effective capacity.** The ratio of actual output for a process to its effective capacity is called **efficiency.**

WORKED EXAMPLE

An Indian car manufacturer has a painting line with a design capacity of 100 square metres per minute and the line is operated 24 hours a day, 7 days a week (168 hours). Design capacity is:

100×60 min/hr $\times 168$ hrs/wk = 1,008,000 square metres per week

Records for a week show the following lost time in production:

1	Product changeovers (set-ups)	18 hrs
2	Regular maintenance	12 hrs
3	No work scheduled	6 hrs
4	Quality sampling checks	8 hrs
5	Shift change times	8 hrs
6	Maintenance breakdown	16 hrs
7	Quality failure investigation	12 hrs
8	Paint stock-outs	6 hrs
9	Labour shortages	6 hrs
10	Waiting for paint	5 hrs
	Total	100 hrs

During this week, production was only $100 \times 60 \times (168 - 100) = 408,000$ square metres per week. The first five categories of lost production are planned occurrences, whilst the last five are unplanned losses.

Design capacity = 168 hours per week

Effective capacity = 168 − 55 = 113 hours per week

Actual output = 168 − 55 − 45 = 68 hours per week

Utilisation $= \dfrac{Actual\ output}{Design\ capacity} = \dfrac{68}{168} = 0.405\ (40\%)$

Efficiency $= \dfrac{Actual\ output}{Effective\ capacity} = \dfrac{68}{113} = 0.602\ (60\%)$

Overall equipment effectiveness (OEE)

OEE is an increasingly popular measure of judging the effectiveness of operations equipment. The OEE is calculated by multiplying an availability rate (a) by a performance rate (p) by a quality rate (q).

$$\textbf{Availability rate } (a) = \frac{Total\ operating\ time}{Loading\ time}$$

Total operating time = Loading time − (Not worked unplanned + Set-up + Breakdown)
Loading time = Original planned operating time of a machine

$$\text{Performance rate } (p) = \frac{Net\ operating\ time}{Total\ operating\ time}$$

Net operating time = Total operating time – Speed losses
Speed losses = Idling + Slow running equipment percentage

$$\text{Quality rate } (q) = \frac{Valuable\ opeating\ time}{Net\ operating\ time}$$

Valuable operating time = Net operating time – Quality losses

---

WORKED EXAMPLE

In a typical 7-day period, the planning department programs a machine for 148 hours – its loading time. Changeovers and set-ups take 8 hours and breakdowns average 4 hours each week. Waiting for materials to be delivered constitutes 6 hours in which the machine cannot work. When the machine is running, it averages 87% of its rated speed. After production, 2% of the parts processed are found to be defective. We can use this information to calculate OEE as follows:

Loading time = 148 hrs
Availability losses = (0 hrs × not worked unplanned) + (8 hrs set-up) + (4 hrs breakdown)
So, total operating time = 148 – 12 = 136 hrs

Speed losses = (6 hrs idling) + ((136 – 6) × 0.13 slow running) = 6 + 16.9 = 22.9 hrs
So, net operating time = 136 – 22.9 = 113.1 hrs

Quality losses = (113.1 net operating time) × (0.02 error rate) = 2.26 hrs
So, valuable operating time = 113.1 – 2.26 = 110.84 hrs

$$\textbf{Availability rate} = \frac{Total\ operating\ time}{Loading\ time} = \frac{136}{148} = 0.9189 = 91.89\%$$

$$\textbf{Performance rate} = \frac{Net\ operating\ time}{Total\ operating\ time} = \frac{113.1}{136} = 0.8316 = 83.16\%$$

$$\textbf{Quality rate} = \frac{Valuable\ operating\ time}{Net\ operating\ time} = \frac{110.84}{113.1} = 0.9797 = 97.97\%$$

OEE = $a \times p \times q$ = 0.9189 × 0.8316 × 0.9797 = 0.7486 = 74.86%

Calculating requirements – single product/service

Once a manager has a demand forecast, this has to be converted to a number that can be compared directly with the capacity measure being used. When one product/service is being delivered (i.e. a single process), capacity required is calculated as follows:

$$\text{Machines/servers required } (M) = \frac{Process\ hours\ required\ for\ annual\ demand}{Hours\ available\ from\ one\ machine\ or\ server - Desired\ cushion}$$

$$= \frac{Dp}{N[1-(C/100)]}$$

Where D = number of forecast units (customers) per annum
p = processing time in hours per unit (or customer)
N = total processing hours per annum
C = desired capacity cushion

WORKED EXAMPLE

Bill Gerhard wants to calculate how many servers are required in his coffee shop. He operates 313 days a year for 11 hours each day. Bill wants a capacity cushion of 12% to deal with unexpected fluctuations in demand. This year Bill is forecasting 500,000 customers with an average processing time of 3 minutes.

$$\text{Servers required } (M) = \frac{\textit{Process hours required for annual demand}}{\textit{Hours available from one machine or server} - \textit{Desired cushion}}$$

$$= \frac{Dp}{N[1-(C/100)]} = \frac{500,000 \times 0.05}{(11 \times 313)[1-(12/100)]} = \frac{25,000}{3,443 \times 0.88} = 8.25$$

Rounding up to the next integer gives a server requirement of 9 staff.

Calculating requirements – multiple products/services

If there are multiple products or services to be delivered, extra time is usually required to switch between one product or service and another. The set-up time is the time taken to change a machine (or server) from making one product/service to another. The total number of set-ups per year is found by dividing forecast demand (D) by the number produced in each lot. This can then be multiplied by set-up time to give a total set-up time per year. For example, if annual demand (D) is 4,000 units and the average lot size is 400, there are 4,000/400 = 10 set-ups per year. Accounting for multiple products with set-up time, we get the following equation:

$$\text{Machines/servers required } (M) = \frac{\begin{array}{c}\textit{Process hours AND set-up hours required for}\\\textit{annual demand, summed over all products}\end{array}}{\begin{array}{c}\textit{Hours available from one machine or server} -\\\textit{Desired cushion}\end{array}}$$

$$= \frac{[Dp+(D/Q)s]\,product\,1+[Dp+(D/Q)s]\,product\,2+\cdots+[Dp+(D/Q)s]\,product\,n}{N[1-(C/100)]}$$

Where Q = number of units in each lot
s = set-up time (in hours) per lot
D = number of forecast units (customers) per annum
p = processing time in hours per unit (or customer)
N = total processing hours per annum
C = desired capacity cushion

WORKED EXAMPLE

Hard Knot Walking Boots Inc. currently has six machines which operate a 12-day shift, 300 days per annum, producing two types of walking boots – the Himalayan and the Andes. The firm has a capacity cushion of 10%. Based on the information below, we can determine how many machines will be needed for the coming year.

	Himalayan	Andes
(D) Demand (units/customers per annum)	36,000	25,000
(p) Processing time (hours per unit/customer)	0.25	0.500
(Q) Number of units in each lot	60	40
(s) Set-up time (hours per lot)	0.2	0.3

$$\text{Machines required } (M) = \frac{\text{Process hours AND set-up hours required for annual demand,}}{\text{Hours available from one machine or server} - \text{desired cushion}}$$

$$= \frac{[Dp+(D/Q)s]product\,1+[Dp+(D/Q)s]product\,2+\cdots+[Dp+(D/Q)s]product\,n}{N[1-(C/100)]}$$

$$= \frac{[36,000(0.25)+(36,000/60)0.20]Himalayan+[25,000(0.5)+(25,000/40)0.30]K^2}{3,600[1-(10/100)]}$$

$$= \frac{9,120+12,687.50}{3,600\times0.9} = \frac{21,807.5}{3,240} = 6.73 \ldots \text{ so we need 7 machines to meet demand.}$$

Questions

2.3.1 A trainer manufacturer produces three types of trainer in its factory – *Basis*, *Flash* and *Gold Rush*. *Basis* can be assembled in 1.5 minutes, *Flash* in 2 minutes and *Gold Rush* in 3 minutes. There are 700 assembly hours available each week. If demand for *Basis*, *Flash* and *Gold Rush* is in a ratio of 6:5:3, how long does it take to assemble 14 units and how many units are produced per week?

2.3.2 If demand for *Basis*, *Flash* and *Gold Rush* changes to a ratio of 2:3:7, how long will it take to produce 12 units and how many units will be produced per week?

2.3.3 If an operation was designed to process 65,000 customer orders per annum, but because of labour shortages and input errors is limited to 52,000 orders per annum, what is the utilisation?

2.3.4 A school canteen has a design capacity of 2,750 meals per week, an effective capacity of 2,460 meals per week, and an efficiency of 82%. How many meals are actually delivered each week?

2.3.5 The design capacity, effective capacity and efficiency for a car licensing operation are shown in the following table:

Process	Design capacity	Effective capacity	Efficiency
Document checking	145,000	128,000	.95
Licence production	1,250,000	900,000	.15
Distribution	165,000	160,000	.75

(a) What are the expected output levels for each process?
(b) What are the utilisation rates for each process?

2.3.6 A camera production facility in Seoul, South Korea has a design capacity of 36,000 cameras per week and the line is operated 16 hours per day, 6 days per week. Records for a week show the following lost time in production:

1	Product changeovers (set-ups)	14 hrs
2	Regular maintenance	6 hrs
3	Quality sampling checks	7 hrs
4	Shift change times	6 hrs
5	Maintenance breakdown	12 hrs
6	Quality failure investigation	7 hrs
7	Material stock-outs	4 hrs
8	Labour shortages	4 hrs
	Total	60 hrs

(a) What was the actual production this week?
(b) Assuming categories 1–4 are planned, what is effective capacity?
(c) What is the utilisation of the facility?
(d) What is the efficiency of the facility?

2.3.7 If the camera production facility is able to reduce all categories of loss by 3 hours,

(a) What is the new level of weekly production?
(b) What is effective capacity?
(c) What is the utilisation of the facility?
(d) What is the efficiency of the facility?

2.3.8 A capping machine in a glass bottling plant based in Poland has a loading time of 152 hours per week. Each week, set-ups average 9 hours, breakdowns 3 hrs and unplanned downtime (no work) 2 hours. The machine lies idle for 4 hours each week whilst waiting for materials to be delivered. When the machine is running, it averages 89% of its rated speed and, after production, 4% of the parts processed are found to be defective. What are the availability, performance, quality rates and the overall equipment effectiveness?

2.3.9 The Kosnos glass bottling plant is looking to reduce set-up time to 6 hrs per week; breakdowns to 1 hr per week; and to improve machine running to 94% of its rated speed. What would be the effect on availability, performance and quality rates, and on total OEE?

2.3.10 A photocopier in a law firm has a loading time of 48 hours per week. Each week, changeovers for new toner average 30 minutes, breakdowns average 1 hour and 30 minutes and unplanned downtime averages 1 hour. The machine lies idle for an average of 45 minutes each week while waiting for materials to be delivered. When the machine is running, it averages 78% of its rated speed and, after photocopying, 15% of the copies are rejected owing to some defect. What are the availability, performance, quality rates and the overall equipment effectiveness?

2.3.11 A dice-making facility in Northern Mexico operates 360 days per annum for an average of 22 hours each day. The operation has a forecast demand of 14 million dice and a single machine can produce a die every 18 seconds. As demand is quite predictable, the facility only requires a cushion of 7%. How many machines are required to meet demand?

2.3.12 If the dice factory's demand actually reaches 15 million, and owing to an industrial dispute is able to operate for only 350 days, how many machines would now be required to meet demand?

2.3.13 A tax office in Barcelona, Spain, operates 8 hours per day for 240 days a year. A tax officer can process one tax return every 24 minutes and annual demand is forecast to be 15,000 returns. The operation has a capacity cushion of 15%. How may tax officers are required to meet demand?

2.3.14 Alpha Accounting currently has five accountants working an 8-hour day, 240 days per annum, working on simple and complex customer accounts. The firm has a capacity cushion of 10%. Based on the information below, do they have enough accountants to meet forecast demand for the coming year?

	Simple	Complex
(D) Demand (customers per annum)	6,500	2,500
(p) Processing time (hours per customer)	0.7	1.5
(Q) Number of units in each lot	8	5
(s) Set-up time (hours per lot)	0.05	0.05

2.3.15 What if Alpha Accounting experience demand for simple accounts of 5,000, but complex account demand increases to 4,000?

2.3.16 Fabrice is a fabric-dyeing operation based in Vietnam producing 3 types of dyed fabric – Purple haze, Blue clouds and Red stripe. It operates 350 days per annum in two 8-hour shifts per day. The firm has a capacity cushion of 6%. Based on the information below, how many dyeing machines are needed to meet forecast demand for the coming year?

	Purple haze	Blue clouds	Red stripe
(D) Demand (metres per annum)	500,000	750,000	250,000
(p) Processing time (hours per metre)	0.05	0.03	0.05
(Q) Number of metres in each lot	500	600	300
(s) Set-up time (hours per lot)	0.75	0.5	1.2

2.3.17 Dove Hernia Trust carries out three types of hernia operation – abdominal hernias, diaphragmatic hernias and pelvic hernias. It carries out operations on Mondays, Wednesdays and Fridays for 6 hrs each day, operates 50 weeks per year and has a capacity cushion of 12%. Based on the following information, how many surgeons are needed to meet forecast demand?

	Abdominal	Diaphragmatic	Pelvic
(D) Demand (operations per annum)	1,200	250	110
(p) Processing time (hours per operation)	1.2	2.3	2.9
(Q) Number of operations in each batch	4	2	1
(s) Set-up time (hours per batch)	0.25	0.3	0.4

2.4 Work measurement

Whilst the scientific management approach to job design has been widely criticised, many of its ideas are still used in modern business. In this section we examine the use of **time studies, sample size calculation,** and **work sampling** as techniques that can be used to determine how long jobs should take to perform and the samples needed to ensure these measurements are reliable.

Time studies

The most popular work measurement technique in operations management is **time studies.** The procedure involves timing a sample of a worker's performance and using it to define a standard task time. These standard times can be combined to calculate the total standard time for a series of tasks.

To calculate **basic time (normal time)** we use the following equation:

Basic time = (Average observed time) × (Performance rating factor)

We can then calculate standard time. This is an adjustment to basic time that takes into account allowances, such as unavoidable delays, worker fatigue and personal needs. **Standard time** is calculated as follows:

$$Standard\ time = \frac{Basic\ time}{1 - Allowance\ factor}$$

WORKED EXAMPLE

A time study showed that the average time taken to deal with car insurance requests by call centre workers in Mumbai, India was 6 minutes. The analyst rated the observed worker at 90%, meaning the worker performed at 90% of basic time when the observations were made. The firm has an allowance factor of 8%. We can calculate the basic and standard time for the operation as follows:

Basic Time = (Average observed time) × (Performance rating factor)

$= 6.0 \times .90 = 5.40$ minutes

$$Standard\ time = \frac{Basic\ time}{1 - Allowance\ factor} = \frac{5.40}{1 - 0.08} = 5.87$$

Sample size calculation

Time studies require a sampling process, so the issue of error naturally arises. To determine an adequate sample size, we must consider 3 issues:

1 level of accuracy required (e.g. ±5%)
2 level of confidence required (e.g. 95%)
3 level of variation in the data (the more variation, the larger the sample needed).

We can calculate the sample size as follows:

$$\text{Required sample size } = \ n = \left(\frac{zs}{h\bar{x}}\right)^2$$

Where h = accuracy level in percent of the job element expressed as a decimal

z = confidence level in standard deviations (e.g. 95% = 1.96)

s = standard deviation of initial sample

$\bar{x}$ = mean of initial sample

n = required sample size

Common z values

Confidence level (%)	z-value (standard deviations for desired confidence level)
90.0	1.65
95.0	1.96
95.45	2.00
99.0	2.58
99.73	3.00

WORKED EXAMPLE

Jacksonville Shoes needs to determine the sample size needed for a future work study. A previous work study has a standard deviation in the sample of 2.0 and a mean of 7.00. Accuracy must be within 5% with a 90% level of confidence. This information allows us to calculate the required sample size as follows:

$z = 1.65 \ s = 2.00 \ h = 0.05 \ \bar{x} = 7.00$

$$\text{Required sample size } = \ n = \left(\frac{zs}{h\bar{x}}\right)^2 = \left(\frac{1.65 \times 2.00}{0.05 \times 7.00}\right)^2 = 88.90 \approx 89$$

Work sampling

An alternative method for developing standard times is called **work sampling**. This technique creates an estimate of the percent of time a worker will take on various tasks. Work sampling follows four steps:

1 a preliminary sample to obtain an estimate of the parameter (e.g. % of idle worker time)
2 sample size requirement calculation
3 observe worker activities randomly
4 determine how workers spend their time (usually as a percent).

In work sampling, sample size required (n) is calculated as follows:

$$n = \frac{z^2 p(1-p)}{h^2}$$

Where z = confidence level in standard deviations (e.g. 95% = 1.96)
h = accuracy level required in percent
p = estimated value of sample proportion (e.g. of idle worker time)

WORKED EXAMPLE

The manager of Hair in Nairobi, Kenya estimates his employees are idle 30% of the time. He wants to take a work sample that is accurate within 5% with a 95% confidence level. Sample size required (n) is calculated as follows:

$$n = \frac{z^2 p(1-p)}{h^2} = n = \frac{(1.96)^2(0.3)(0.7)}{(0.05)^2} = 322.69 \approx 323$$

Questions

2.4.1   A time study showed that the average time taken to carry out an eye examination in a hospital based in Copenhagen is 11 minutes. What is standard time assuming the analyst rated the observed worker at 78% and the firm has an allowance factor of 10% for this operation?

2.4.2   A time study of workers in a glass factory in Hungary showed that the average time taken to blow a vase was 6 minutes. Assuming the analyst rated the observed workers at 120% (i.e. they are working 20% faster than they would be expected to under normal conditions) and the firm has an allowance factor of 15%, what is the standard time for this operation?

2.4.3   Workers in a sandwich-making operation take an average of 5 minutes to make a batch of 10 sandwiches. Given a performance rating of 7% and an allowance of 10%, what is the standard time for the process?

2.4.4   Jacqueline Mulvaney makes designer corsages for sale in the UK and USA. Her husband, Jonathan, has carried out a quick time study so she is able to accurately assess how much work she can take on in any month. Given an allowance factor of 10%, work out the basic times for each element and the standard time for the whole corsage-making process.

Job element	\multicolumn{6}{c}{Observations (minutes)}	Rating
	1	2	3	4	5	6	Rating
Fabric cutting	10.0	12.0	15.0	9.0	8.0	12.0	1.20
Stitching	15.0	22.0	20.0	18.0	12.0	15.0	0.90
Packaging	2.0	2.5	2.5	3.0	1.5	2.0	0.85

2.4.5   A cleaning contractor working for a university in Capetown, South Africa wants to calculate the standard time for cleaning an office on campus. Given an allowance factor of 15%, what is the standard time for the whole operation?

Job element	1	2	3	4	5	6	7	Rating
Empty bins	1.000	0.900	0.750	1.200	1.400	0.600	0.800	0.900
Vacuum floor	3.000	4.500	4.000	3.500	3.000	3.750	4.250	1.250

2.4.6   A previous work study at W.H. Hardy had a standard deviation in the sample of 155 and a mean of 500. Given that accuracy must be within 5% with a 99% level of confidence, what sample size is required for a future work study?

2.4.7   A previous work study for Columbia University library book withdrawals had a standard deviation in the sample of 0.8 minutes and a mean of 1.8 minutes. Given that accuracy must be within 10% with a 90% level of confidence, what sample size is required for a future work study?

2.4.8   An analyst has taken 100 observations of workers at J.R. Hope Ltd. The average observed time is 12 minutes with a standard deviation of 3.56 minutes. Is this sample large enough for the firm to be 95% confident that the standard time is within 5% of the true value? If not, what is the required sample size?

2.4.9   Accurite Watch Repairs has studied a worker 5 times in anticipation of introducing a new job design to the shop floor. What sample (to the nearest whole number) is needed for the firm to be 99% confident that the standard time is within 4% of the true value?

Observation	Time (min)
1	2.60
2	2.90
3	2.20
4	3.00
5	3.30

2.4.10 The manager of Blacks Camping estimates her workers are idle 25% of the time. She wants to take a work sample that is accurate within 10%, but with a 99% confidence level. What sample size is required?

2.4.11 What sample size is required if the manager wants to ensure that the sample is accurate within 5% instead of 10%?

2.4.12 A preliminary study in a shoe shop suggests that workers are active for 85% of the time. What is the required work sample for a sample that will be accurate within 3%, with a 90% confidence level?

2.4.13 Based on 50 observations of staff at a car rental garage in Athens, Greece, the manager concludes that her employees are idle for 30% of the time. If the manager wants a confidence level of 95% and if 10% is an acceptable error, is the sample size large enough? If not, how large should it be?

2.5   Failure, reliability and redundancy

Operations need to have plans to recover from failures or mitigate their effects. However, it is clearly better to prevent failures occurring in the first place. Therefore, we need to measure how likely a failure is to occur and the impact that building redundancy into the system has on this.

Failure rate

The **failure rate** (**FR**) is a measure of failure defined as the number of failures over a period of time. It can be measured as a percentage or as a number of failures over time using the following equations:

$$FR^{\%} = \frac{Number\ of\ failures}{Total\ number\ of\ products\ tested} \times 100$$

or in time

$$FR^{time} = \frac{Number\ of\ failures}{Operating\ time}$$

WORKED EXAMPLE

150 bed mattresses are tested for 3,000 hours. Three fail during the test as follows:

Failure 1 at 950 hours
Failure 2 at 1,250 hours
Failure 3 at 1,800 hours

The failure rate, as a percentage, is:

$$\frac{Number\ of\ failures}{Total\ number\ of\ products\ tested} \times 100 = \frac{3}{150} \times 100 = 2\%$$

The total test time = 150 × 3,000 = 450,000 component hours. However, operating test time must deduct the non-operating time for the three failed components. So

Operating time = 450,000 − [(3,000 − 950) + (3,000 − 1,250) + (3,000 − 1,800)] = 445,000

Failure rate, in time is: $FR^{time} = \dfrac{Number\ of\ failures}{Operating\ time} = \dfrac{3}{445,000} = 0.0000067$

Mean time between failures (MTBF)

A popular alternative measure of failure is the **mean time between failures** (**MTBF**). This is the reciprocal of the failure rate (in time) and is calculated as:

$$MTBF = \frac{1}{Number\ of\ failures}$$

WORKED EXAMPLE

So for our bed mattress example, above, given a failure rate of 0.0000067 failures per hour, the *MTBF* is:

$$\frac{1}{0.0000067} = 149,253.73$$

So, we can expect one mattress to fail every 149,253.73 hours.

Reliability

When used in relation to failure, the term **reliability** means the ability of a system, product or service to perform as expected over time and is usually given as a probability of success. Assuming a system has n interdependent components each with their own reliability, R_1, R_2, $R_{3...}R_n$, the reliability of the whole system, R_s, is:

$$R_s = R_1 \times R_2 \times R_3 \times ... R_n$$

WORKED EXAMPLE

An automated sandwich-making machine in a food manufacturer's factory has six major components, with individual reliabilities as follows:

Bread slicer	Reliability: 0.97
Butter applicator	Reliability: 0.96
Salad filler	Reliability: 0.94
Meat filler	Reliability: 0.92
Top slice of bread applicator	Reliability: 0.96
Wrapper	Reliability: 0.91

If one of these parts of the production line fails, the system will stop working. Therefore, the reliability of the whole system is:

R_s = 0.97 × 0.96 × 0.94 × 0.92 × 0.96 × 0.91 = 0.704

Redundancy

In many operations it is important to build in **redundancy**, components of processes, products, or services that are only used if other components fail. Having such back-up systems naturally adds costs, so it is generally used when a breakdown could have a critical impact on the operation. The reliability of components R_a and R_b working in parallel, R_{a+b}, is calculated as:

$$R_{a+b} = R_a + [(R_b) \times (1 - R_a)]$$

WORKED EXAMPLE

The owner of the factory above has decided that the wrapper in the automated sandwich-making machine is too unreliable and she needs a second wrapper which will come into action if the first one fails. The two wrappers (each with reliability of 0.91) working together have a reliability of:

0.91 + [0.91 × (1 − 0.91)] = 0.99

The reliability of the whole machine is now:

0.97 × 0.96 × 0.94 × 0.92 × 0.96 × 0.99 = 0.765

Worked example *continued*

Clearly, a component will be even more reliable if there is more than one back-up. For example, if we have three components working in parallel with the following reliabilities:

$R_1 = 0.9\ R_2 = 0.8\ R_3 = 0.7$

we can calculate the reliability of the components R_1 and R_2 and R_3 working in parallel, R_{1+2+3}, as:

$R_{1+2+3} = R_1 + \left[(R_2) \times (1 - R_1)\right] + \left[(R_3) \times (1 - R_{1+2})\right]$

$R_{1+2+3} = 0.90 + \left[(0.8) \times (1 - 0.90)\right] + \left[(0.7) \times (1 - 0.98)\right] = 0.90 + 0.08 + 0.014 = .994a$

Availability

When an operation has either failed or is being repaired following a failure, it is unavailable. As such, **availability** is the degree to which the operation is ready to work. When it is being used to indicate operating time excluding the consequence of failure, availability is calculated as follows:

$$Availability\ (A) = \frac{MTBF}{MTBF + MTTR}$$

Where $MTBF$ = mean time between failures
$MTTR$ = mean time to repair

WORKED EXAMPLE

A cardboard compactor at a recycling depot in Alborg, Denmark is proving problematic. Currently, the mean time between failures of the machine is 120 hours and its mean time to repair is 8 hours. Therefore:

$$Availability\ (A) = \frac{MTBF}{MTBF + MTTR} = \frac{120}{120 + 8} = 0.938$$

The depot has worked out two alternative service deals. One option is to use preventative maintenance which would be carried out every three weeks. This would raise the *MTBF* of the compactor to 150 hours. The other option is to employ a faster repair service which would reduce the *MTTR* to 6 hours. Both options cost the same amount. Which would give the depot the higher availability?

$$Availability^{preventative} = \frac{MTBF}{MTBF + MTTR} = \frac{150}{150 + 8} = 0.949$$

$$Availability^{fast\ repair} = \frac{MTBF}{MTBF + MTTR} = \frac{120}{120 + 6} = 0.952$$

So, availability would be greater if the depot employed a faster repair service.

2.5.1   Over an 8-hour period a manager at Taco Bell checks the accuracy of orders delivered to customers. Of 2,800 meals delivered, 21 are not delivered to specification. What is the failure rate as a percentage?

2.5.2   160 toilets for the Airbus A380 are tested for 5,000 hours each. Two fail – one at 120 hours, the other at 350 hours. What is the failure rate, as a percentage in numbers per hour?

2.5.3   A batch of 100 microchips is tested for 1,500 hours. Four of the components fail during the test at 1,105 hours, 1,255 hours, 1,340 hours and 1,435 hours. What is the failure rate as a percentage, the total non-operating time, and the *MTBF*?

2.5.4   A batch of 35 radio components is tested for 800 hours. Five of the components fail during the test at 260, 375, 410, 720 and 780 hours.

(a) What is the failure rate as a percentage?
(b) What is the total non-operating time?
(c) What is the failure rate in time?
(d) What is the *MTBF* for the component?

2.5.5   A batch of 60 calculators is tested for 1,200 hours. Failures occur at 635, 710, 990 and 1,150 hours.

(a) What is the failure rate as a percentage?
(b) What is the total non-operating time?
(c) What is the failure rate in time?
(d) What is the *MTBF* for the component?

2.5.6   An automated shirt-making machine in a clothes manufacturer's factory has four major components, with individual reliabilities as follows:

Shape cutter   Reliability: 0.92   Seam stitcher   Reliability: 0.90
Button applicator Reliability: 0.95   Wrapper   Reliability: 0.97

(a) What is the reliability of the whole system?
(b) If the owner of the factory decided to employ a second seam stitcher which would come into action when the first one failed, what would the seam stitchers' reliability be?
(c) What would the reliability of the whole machine then be?

2.5.7   An automated shampoo-bottling machine in a manufacturer's factory has four major components, with individual reliabilities as follows:

Bottle moulder   Reliability: 0.89   Bottle filler   Reliability: 0.96
Lid applicator   Reliability: 0.93   Labeller   Reliability: 0.94

(a) What is the reliability of the whole system?
(b) If the operations manager had a back-up bottle moulder, what would the bottle moulders' reliability be?
(c) What would the reliability of the whole machine then be?

2.5.8   John Oats has a system composed of three components in parallel. The components have the following reliabilities:

$$R_1 = 0.90 \qquad R_2 = 0.95 \qquad R_3 = 0.85$$

What is the reliability of the system (*Hint*: remember this is in parallel, not in series)?

2.5.9   A mail-sorting machine at a regional mail-sorting office in Coventry is regularly failing. Currently, the mean time between failures of the machine is 24 hours and its mean time to repair is 3 hours. What is its availability?

2.5.10 The sorting office has worked out two alternative service deals. One option is to use preventative maintenance which would be carried out every week. This would raise the *MTBF* of the printer to 28 hours. The other option is to employ a faster repair service which would reduce the *MTTR* to 2 hours. Both options cost the same amount. Which would give the depot the higher availability?

2.5.11 An automated pizza oven at a large pizza chain keeps breaking down. Currently, the mean time between failures of the machine is 16 hours and its mean time to repair is 2 hours. What is its availability?

2.5.12 The pizza chain has the option to use preventative maintenance to raise *MTBF* to 22 hours or train staff to repair the oven and so reduce *MTTR* to 1.5 hours. Which is the better option given the costs are the same?

2.6 Statistical process control

Statistical process control (SPC) is concerned with checking a product or service during its creation. If there is reason to believe that there is a problem with the process, it can be stopped and the problem identified and rectified. The first step in SPC is to set upper and lower control limits, using different techniques depending on what is being controlled – attributes or variables. We can then examine whether a process is in control or not, often termed 'process capability'.

Control charts for attributes

Attributes only have two states – 'right' and 'wrong' for example. There are two types of attribute control charts – **p charts** measure the *percent* of 'wrongs' in a sample, **c charts** measure the *number* of wrongs in a sample.

For p charts, one standard deviation of the distribution of 'wrongs' in a sample (σ_p) is given as:

$$\sigma_p = \sqrt{\frac{\overline{p}(1-\overline{p})}{n}}$$

Where $\overline{p}$ = average percentage of 'wrongs' in the population

n = sample size of *each* sample

p-chart upper and lower control limits can then be set as follows:

$$UCL_p = \overline{p} + z\sigma_p$$

$$LCL_p = \overline{p} - z\sigma_p$$

Where z = number of standard deviations (most common is $z = 3$ for 99.73% limit)

For c charts, one standard deviation of the distribution of 'wrongs' in a sample (σ_c) is given as:

$$\sigma_c = \sqrt{\bar{c}}$$

Where $\bar{c}$ = mean number of defects per unit

Assuming 99.73% control limits for a c chart (3 standard deviations), upper and lower control limits can then be set as follows:

$$UCL_c = \bar{c} + 3\sigma_c$$

$$LCL_c = \bar{c} - 3\sigma_c$$

WORKED EXAMPLE

An animal park in San Diego, USA samples 50 visitors each day (n) to see how many visitors are from overseas. The data below is for the last 7 days.

1	7
2	8
3	12
4	5
5	5
6	4
7	8

p-chart control limits ($z = \pm 3\sigma$) can be calculated as follows:

$$\sigma_p = \sqrt{\frac{\bar{p}(1 - \bar{p})}{n}} = \sqrt{\frac{0.14(1 - 0.14)}{50}} = 0.049$$

$$UCL_p = \bar{p} + z\sigma_p = 0.14 + (3 \times 0.049) = 0.287$$

$$LCL_p = \bar{p} - z\sigma_p = 0.14 - (3 \times 0.049) = -0.007 = 0 \text{ because we can't have a negative control limit}$$

c-chart control limits ($z = \pm 3\sigma$) can be calculated as follows:

$$\sigma_c = \sqrt{\bar{c}} = \sqrt{7} = 2.646$$

$$UCL_c = \bar{c} + 3\sigma_c = 7.0 + (3 \times 2.646) = 14.938$$

$$LCL_c = \bar{c} - 3\sigma_c = 7.0 - (3 \times 2.646) = -0.938 = 0 \text{ because we can't have a negative control limit}$$

Control charts for variables

Unlike attributes, variables have continuous dimensions – e.g. weight, size, height, speed. The most common method for controlling variables is the $\bar{X} - R$ **chart**. The $\bar{X}$ chart measures changes in the mean, whilst the R chart measures changes in the range of values. The first task in calculating variable control limits is to estimate the population mean and average range:

$$\overline{\overline{X}} = \frac{\overline{X}_1 + \overline{X}_2 + ... + \overline{X}_n}{m}$$

$$\overline{R} = \frac{R_1 + R_2 + ... + R_n}{m}$$

Where $\overline{\overline{X}}$ = population mean (mean of sample means)

$\overline{X}$ = sample mean

m = number of samples

n = sample size of *each* sample

$\overline{R}$ = average range of samples

R = sample range

We can then calculate the upper and lower control limits for the sample means chart:

$$UCL = \overline{\overline{X}} + A_2 \overline{R}$$

$$LCL = \overline{\overline{X}} - A_2 \overline{R}$$

And for the range chart:

$$UCL = D_4 \overline{R}$$

$$LCL =$$

The factors, A_2, D_3 and D_4 vary with sample size and are shown in the table below:

Factors for the calculation of control limits

Sample size n	A_2	D_3	D_4
2	1.880	0	3.267
3	1.023	0	2.575
4	0.729	0	2.282
5	0.577	0	2.115
6	0.483	0	2.004
7	0.419	0.076	1.924
8	0.373	0.136	1.864
9	0.337	0.184	1.816
10	0.308	0.223	1.777
12	0.266	0.284	1.716
14	0.235	0.329	1.671
16	0.212	0.364	1.636
18	0.194	0.392	1.608
20	0.180	0.414	1.586
22	0.167	0.434	1.566
24	0.157	0.452	1.548

Source: Slack, N., Chambers, S. and Johnston, R. (2007) *Operations Management*, Fifth Edition, Harlow, England: Pearson Financial Times Prentice Hall, Table 17.6, p. 563. Reproduced by permission

WORKED EXAMPLE

The manager of a sweet shop in Perth, Austrlia decides to sample batches of sweets to check that the weight is reasonably consistent. She takes 9 samples, each with 10 bags. The data below shows the average mean weight for each sample and the weight range.

Sample	Weight average in grams $\bar{x}$	Range (R)
1	10	1.50
2	8	2.00
3	9	3.00
4	9	2.50
5	8	1.50
6	9	1.00
7	11	2.00
8	14	2.50
9	12	2.00

We can calculate the population mean (i.e. the average mean) as follows:

$$\bar{\bar{X}} = \frac{\bar{X}_1 + \bar{X}_2 + ... + \bar{X}_n}{m} = \frac{10+8+9+9+8+9+11+14+12}{9} = \frac{90}{9} = 10.0$$

$$\bar{R} = \frac{R_1 + R_2 + ... + R_n}{m} = \frac{1.5+2+3+2.5+1.5+1+2+2.5+2}{9} = \frac{18}{9} = 2.0$$

Using the factors table, we can then calculate the upper and lower control limits for the sample means chart:

$$UCL = \bar{\bar{X}} + A_2\bar{R} = 10.0 + (0.308 \times 2.0) = 10.616$$

$$LCL = \bar{\bar{X}} - A_2\bar{R} = 10.0 - (0.308 \times 2.0) = 9.384$$

We can also calculate the upper and lower controls for the range chart:

$$UCL = D_4\bar{R} = 1.777 \times 2.0 = 3.554$$

$$LCL = D_3\bar{R} = 0.223 \times 2.0 = 0.446$$

Process capability

Process capability is a measure of process variation acceptability. The simplest measure of capability (C_p) is the ratio of the specification range to the natural process variation (i.e. ± 3 standard deviations):

$$C_p = \frac{UTL - LTL}{6s}$$

Where UTL = upper control limit
LTL = lower control limit
s = standard deviation of the process variability

As a general rule, if C_p is greater than 1, the process is said to be 'capable' and if it is less than 1, it is said to be 'incapable'. When process average is offset from the specification (i.e. to the left or right), we use **one-sided** capability indices to assess process capability:

$$Upper\ one\text{-}sided\ index\ \ C_{pu} = \frac{UTL - X}{3s}$$

$$Lower\ one\text{-}sided\ index\ \ C_{pl} = \frac{X - LTL}{3s}$$

Where X = the process average

Sometimes, only the lower (i.e. minimum) of the two one-sided indices is used to indicate process capability. This is called the **process capability index**:

$$C_{pk} = \min\left(C_{pu}, C_{pl}\right)$$

WORKED EXAMPLE

A candle production facility in Bangladesh produces candles with an average burn-time of 45 hours and a standard deviation of 3 hours. The nominal value of the tolerance range is 50 hours with an upper specification of 60 hours and a lower specification of 40 hours. The operations manager wants to determine if the process is 'capable':

$$C_p = \frac{UTL - LTL}{6s} = \frac{60 - 40}{6 \times 3} = 1.11$$

The C_p ratio suggests that the process variability is acceptable relative to the range of tolerance limits (i.e. >1). However, because the average burn-time is not at the mid-point of the specification range, we need to calculate C_{pk}:

$$Upper\ one\text{-}sided\ index\ \ C_{pu} = \frac{UTL - X}{3s} = \frac{60 - 45}{3 \times 3} = 1.67$$

$$Lower\ one\text{-}sided\ index\ \ C_{pl} = \frac{X - LTL}{3s} = \frac{45 - 40}{3 \times 3} = 0.56$$

$$C_{pk} = \min\left(C_{pu}, C_{pl}\right) = 0.56$$

This capability index indicates that the distribution is too close to the lower specification and is in fact 'incapable' (< 1).

2.6.1 A manager takes samples of 1,000 chocolate boxes (n) once a month for nine months. The data below shows the number of defective boxes.

1	15
2	12
3	18
4	8
5	25
6	7
7	3
8	9
9	14

Assuming $z = \pm 3\sigma$, calculate the p-chart and c-chart upper and lower control limits.

2.6.2 Over a 15-week period, a manager takes a weekly sample of 50 insurance claims to check for mistakes. Based on the data below, set p-chart and c-chart control limits to include 99.73% of random variation ($z = \pm 3\sigma$).

1	5
2	8
3	4
4	2
5	6
6	3
7	6
8	5
9	4
10	3
11	7
12	5
13	3
14	2
15	3

2.6.3 A pizza delivery company takes 5 samples of 50 pizzas to check for errors in topping. On average, 10% of all pizzas had some topping error. What are the c-chart control limits to include 99.73% of random variation ($z = \pm 3\sigma$)?

2.6.4 The pizza delivery company decides to take 5 new samples but with 100 pizzas in each sample. This time, there is an average error rate of 13%. What are the c-chart control limits to include 99.73% of random variation ($z = \pm 3\sigma$) for this larger sample size?

2.6.5 A hospital manager has been checking junior doctor records to assess how many errors have been made in patient diagnosis. Of 500 records examined, 25 have some error. Calculate the upper and lower p-chart control limits for 99.73% confidence.

2.6.6 The hospital manager takes a second sample of 500 patient records. In this case, 30 have an error. What is the maximum percentage (UCL) of errors that any further sample could have based on p-chart control limits for a 99.73% confidence?

2.6.7   A manager wants to develop a range chart for a bottling process. He takes 10 samples of 8 batches and finds a mean bottling time of 15.7 minutes per batch, with a range of 3.4 minutes. What are the upper and lower control limits for the range chart?

2.6.8   A logistics manager wants to assess how varied the weight of lorry loads is over a period of time. He takes 5 samples of 20 lorry loads (n) and notes the average load (tonnes) and the range within each sample.

Sample	Weight average in tonnes ($\bar{x}$)	Range (R)
1	15.50	4.50
2	12.30	5.30
3	8.80	6.20
4	10.30	5.20
5	13.10	3.80

(a) What are the population means for the mean and the range?
(b) What are the upper and lower control limits for the sample means chart?
(c) What are the upper and lower controls for the range chart?

2.6.9   A florist located in Ankara, Turkey takes 4 samples of 12 flower bouquets and counts how many flowers are in each bouquet. The total average mean is 19.5 flowers, with a total average range of 6.0 flowers.

(a) What are the upper and lower control limits for the sample means chart?
(b) What are the upper and lower controls for the range chart?

2.6.10 A manager of an insurance department collects six samples of 24 insurance claims and looks at how long each claim took to process. Based on the data below:

(a) What are the upper and lower control limits for the sample means chart?
(b) What are the upper and lower controls for the range chart?

	Sample ave $\bar{x}$	Range (R)
1	28.50	6.75
2	26.25	5.50
3	35.50	8.00
4	22.75	7.25
5	30.75	6.50
6	29.25	6.00

2.6.11 A photography firm based in Tianjin, China specialising in school children's portraits, takes 5 samples of 5 photography job-times (minutes) to examine if the process is in control or not. Based on the following data collected:

(a) What is the average time for sample 2?
(b) What is the range for sample 4?
(c) What is the population mean time and average range?
(d) What are the upper and lower control limits for the sample means chart?
(e) What are the upper and lower controls for the range chart?
(f) Is the process in control?

	Job 1	Job 2	Job 3	Job 4	Job 5
1	20	25	15	18	15
2	25	30	15	20	17
3	16	30	25	24	20
4	39	48	43	37	15
5	17	15	33	35	24

2.6.12 Service agents in a mobile phone shop take an average of 20 minutes to set up a new customer contract, with a standard deviation of 5 minutes. The upper tolerance level is set at 25 minutes and the lower tolerance level at 10 minutes. Calculate the capability ratio (C_p) and the capability index (C_{pk}) to determine if this process is in control.

2.6.13 A manager wants to assess if a mail-sorting machine is capable of performing as expected. The machine currently sorts an average of 4,000 letters an hour, with a standard deviation of 125 letters. The upper tolerance is set at 5,500 and the lower tolerance at 3,500. What is the capability index (C_{pk}) for this machine?

2.6.14 What is the capability index if the machine average falls from 4,000 letters to 3,750?

2.6.15 A heart surgeon working in the Tung Wah Hospital, Hong Kong carries out operations in an average of 3 hours with a standard deviation of 45 minutes. The upper tolerance for this operation type is 5 hours and the lower tolerance is 2 hours. What are the upper and lower one-sided indices?

2.6.16 If the average increased operation time for the heart surgeon increased to 3.5 hours, but the standard deviation dropped to 30 minutes, what would the capability index (C_{pk}) be?

2.7 Little's Law and balancing loss

We now move from descriptive techniques that are used simply to measure what is happening in an operation, to those that describe behaviour in an operation. Remember, in this situation we are seeking to describe the relationships that define process or operations behaviour. **Little's Law** and **balancing loss** are related measures of behaviour that are simple, but also very useful.

Little's Law

Little's Law illustrates the mathematical relationship between **throughput, work-in-progress (WIP)** and **cycle time**. Whilst it is very simple, it works for any stable process.

$$\text{Throughput time} = Work\text{-}in\text{-}progress \times Cycle\ time$$

$$\text{Work-in-progress} = \frac{Throughput\ time}{Cycle\ time}$$

$$\text{Cycle time} = \frac{Throughput\ time}{Work\ in\ progress}$$

$$\text{Servers required} = \frac{Work\ content}{Cycle\ time}$$

WORKED EXAMPLE

At the theatre located in Omsk, Russia, the interval during a performance of *King Lear* lasts for 20 minutes and in that time 86 women need to use the toilet. On average, a woman spends 3 minutes in the cubicle. There are 10 toilets available. Using this information, we can assess if the theatre has enough toilets to deal with the demand.

WIP (demand for toilets) = 86 women
Throughput time (length of interval) = 20 mins
Work content (average time to use the toilet) = 3 mins

$$\text{Cycle time} = \frac{\text{Throughput time}}{\text{WIP}} = \frac{20}{86} = 0.23 \text{ minutes}$$

$$\text{The number of toilets required} = \frac{\text{Work content}}{\text{Cycle time}} = \frac{3}{0.23} = 13.04 \text{ toilets}$$

There are not enough toilets to deal with demand since the theatre has 10 women's toilets and 13.04 are needed. Given the fact that work content (the time taken to use the toilet) cannot realistically be altered, nor WIP (the number of people needing the toilet) be reduced, what are the theatre's options?

1 More toilets – 14 to cover demand
2 A longer interval:

$$\text{(New) cycle time} = \frac{\text{Work content}}{\text{Number of toilets}} = \frac{3}{10} = 0.3$$

Throughput time = WIP × Cycle time = 86 × 0.3 = 25.8 minutes. The interval would need to be 26 minutes to ensure that all demand was met.

Balancing loss

As noted, the cycle time is the average time between units of output emerging from a process. If, for example, a gourmet burger shop has a daily demand for 250 burgers and operates for 10 hours, the required cycle time will be 10/250 = 0.04 hours = 2.4 minutes. So, the shop must be capable of processing a burger once every 2.4 minutes. We also know that the number of servers = work content / cycle time. In this case, assuming that each burger has 7.2 minutes of work required, the number of servers required is 7.2 / 2.4 = 3. This assumes that each server (or stage in a process) contributes an equal amount to the total work content. However, in most cases, work is not perfectly balanced – this is termed **balancing loss**.

WORKED EXAMPLE

A burger outlet in Santa Monica, USA has a 3-stage process for making burgers. Stage 1 takes 2.0 minutes, stage 2 takes 3.0 minutes and stage 3 takes 2.2 minutes. Because of the bottleneck process in stage 2, the cycle time in this case is now 3 minutes. Balancing loss can be calculated as follows:

Idle time every cycle = (3.0 – 2.0) + (3.0 – 0.0) + (3.0 – 2.2) = 1.8 minutes

Balancing loss = 1.8 / (3.0 × 3) = 0.2 = 20%

2.7.1 The Cocoa and Coffee Company always has 3 members of staff serving drinks and snacks. It is open for 10 hours every day and the average time it takes for any customer to be served is 4 minutes. How many customers can they serve in a day?

2.7.2 How many more customers could they serve in a day if they had 5 servers?

2.7.3 If the coffee company keeps the number of staff at 3, improves their efficiency and reduces the average time taken to serve a customer from 4 minutes to 2.5 minutes, how many customers can they serve in a day?

2.7.4 One of the responsibilities of the Jefferson Bank office is to deal with applications from new customers for their credit cards. The number of applications to be processed is 450 per week and the time available to process these is 12 hours per week. What is the required cycle time for the process?

2.7.5 For the office described above, the total work content of all the activities necessary to process an application is, on average, 25 minutes. How many people will be needed to meet the demand?

2.7.6 The same office likes to have all of the desks clear at the end of a shift. How many applications should be loaded onto the process in the morning to ensure that all are completed by the end of a 3-hour shift?

2.7.7 A company that repairs kettles is sent faulty items by customers, tests them, repairs them and returns them to the customer. Although the process varies a little depending on the fault, the repairs take approximately the same time. If the cycle time of the process is 16 minutes and the average work in process is 3 units, presuming there is no space for inventory to build up, then what is the throughput time?

2.7.8 If more difficult problems arise and the cycle time becomes 22 minutes, then what will the throughput time be?

2.7.9 If the cycle time remains at 16 minutes but there is more space for inventory so the work in process becomes 7 units, what will the throughput time be?

2.7.10 An accounting firm based in Galle, Sri Lanka has a 4-stage process for tax returns. Stage 1 takes 15 minutes, stage 2 takes 18 minutes, stage 3 takes 20 minutes and stage 4 takes 13 minutes. What is the idle time in each process cycle and what is the percentage balancing loss?

2.7.11 A Congolese bank has a 5-stage process for new account applications. Based on the following information, what is the idle time in each process cycle and what is the percentage balancing loss?

Stage	Processing time
1	10
2	16
3	22
4	8
5	12

2.7.12 What would the new idle time and balancing loss percentage be if stages 1 and 2, and stages 4 and 5, were combined?

2.8 Queuing methods

Queuing theory helps us to analyse and study queues. The basic phenomenon of queuing arises whenever a shared facility needs to be accessed for services by a large number of jobs or customers. A queue forms when a service request arrives at a service facility and is forced to wait while the server is busy working on other requests.

If 'A' denotes the distribution of arrival times, 'B' denotes the distribution of processing times, 'm' denotes the number of servers at each station and 'b' denotes the maximum number of items allowed in the system, a queuing system can be represented as **A/B/m/b**. Most common distributions used to describe A or B are either exponential (or Markovian) distribution (M) or general (or normal) distribution (G). The result is two common types of queuing system – **M/M/m** and **G/G/m queuing systems**. The simplified form of M/M/m and G/G/m queuing systems are M/M/1 and G/G/1 respectively.

Notation

t_a	= average time between arrival	
r_a	= arrival rate (items per unit time)	$= 1/t_a$
c_a	= coefficient of variation of arrival times	$= \sigma_a/t_a$
σ_a	= standard deviation for arrival time distribution	
m	= number of parallel servers at a station	
t_e	= mean processing time	
r_e	= processing rate (items per unit time)	$= 1/t_e$
c_e	= coefficient of variation of process time	$= \sigma_e/t_e$
σ_e	= standard deviation for processing time distribution	
u	= utilisation of station	
WIP	= average work in progress (number of items) in the queue	
WIP_q	= expected work in progress (number of times) in the queue	
W_q	= expected waiting time in the queue	
W	= expected waiting time in the system (queue time + processing time)	

M/M/m queuing system

M/M/m represents a queuing system with exponential arrival and processing times with 'm' servers and no maximum limit to the queue.

$$u = \frac{r_a}{\left(r_e \times m\right)}$$

$$W_q = \frac{u^{\sqrt{2\,(m+1)}-1}}{m\,(1-u)}\, t_e$$

$$WIP_q = r_a \times W_q$$

WORKED EXAMPLE

Niraj Kumar has recently introduced a new computer simulation game in his entertainment centre called *'cyber game world'*. In a very short time it has gained wide popularity and a queue of kids can be seen who want to try the game. There are 4 stations where the game can be played. On average kids arrive at a rate of 15 per hour and each plays the game for 10 minutes on average. It has been found that the arrival times and processing times are exponentially distributed. The queuing system in this problem is identified as M/M/m type. We can calculate the average waiting time for kids in the queue as follows:

r_a = 15 per hour, therefore
t_a = (1 / 15) hours = (60 / 15) minutes = 4 minutes
t_e = 10 minutes = 10 / 60 = 0.17 hours , therefore
r_e = (1 / 10) per minute = (60 / 10) per hour = 6 per hour
m = 4

Utilisation of station would be:

$$u = \frac{15}{(6 \times 4)} = 0.625$$

Waiting time in queue:

$$W_q = \frac{0.625^{\sqrt{2(4+1)}-1}}{4\,(1-0.625)} \times 0.17$$

$$= \frac{0.625^{\sqrt{10}-1}}{4 \times (0.375)} \times 0.17$$

$$= \frac{0.625^{2.16}}{1.5} \times 0.17$$

$$= \frac{0.36}{1.5} \times 0.17$$

$$= 0.041 \text{ hours}$$

$$= 2.44 \text{ minutes}$$

Therefore the average waiting time would be 2.44 minutes.

M/M/1 queuing system

M/M/1 represents a queuing system with exponential arrival and processing times with only one server and no maximum limit to the queue. This is the simplified form of M/M/m queuing system, when $m = 1$.

$$u = \frac{r_a}{r_e} = r_a t_e$$

$$W_q = \frac{u}{(1-u)} t_e$$

$$WIP_q = \frac{u^2}{1-u}$$

WORKED EXAMPLE

The owner of a resturant in Denpasar, Bali wishes to provide better customer service in terms of reducing the waiting time of customers at the cashier's counter. There is only one cashier counter in the restaurant. After careful analysis of the customers' arrival pattern and queuing system, the manager realises that customers arrive at a rate of 10 per hour and on average the cashier takes 5 minutes to serve one customer. It has also been found that the customer's arrival time and processing time are both exponentially distributed. We can calculate the average waiting time in the queue as follows:

r_a = 10 per hour, therefore
t_a = (1 / 10) hours = (60 / 10) minutes = 6 minutes
t_e = 5 minutes = 5 / 60 = 0.083 hour, therefore
r_e = (1 / 5) per minute = (60 / 5) per hour = 12 per hour

Utilisation of the single cashier counter,

u = 10 / 12 = 0.83

Waiting time in queue,

$$W_q = \frac{0.83}{(1-0.83)} \times 0.083$$

$$= \frac{0.83}{0.17} \times 0.083$$

$$= 0.40 \text{ hour}$$

$$= 24.0 \text{ minutes}$$

Therefore the average waiting time in queue would be 24 minutes.

G/G/m queuing system

G/G/m represents a queuing system with general or normal arrival and processing times with m servers and no maximum limit to the queue.

$$u = \frac{r_a}{\left(r_e \times m\right)}$$

$$W_q = \left(\frac{c_a^2 + c_e^2}{2}\right) \left(\frac{u^{\sqrt{2(m+1)}-1}}{m\,(1-u)}\right) t_e$$

$$WIP_q = r_a \times W_q$$

WORKED EXAMPLE

There are 5 check-out counters at a supermarket in Sao Paulo, Brazil. On average 10 customers arrive in an hour and it takes 14 minutes to serve one customer. It has been found that the customers' arrival times and processing times are normally distributed. We can estimate the average waiting time in the queue, when the following data is also provided:

■ The coefficient of variation of customer arrival time = 1.5
■ The coefficient of variation of processing time = 3.0

Worked example *continued*

$c_a = 1.5$

$c_e = 3.0$

$r_a = 10$ per hour, therefore,

$t_a = (1 / 10)$ hours $= 0.1$ hours $= 6$ minutes

$t_e = 14$ minutes $= 0.23$ hours, therefore,

$r_e = (1/ 0.23)$ per hour $= 4.35$ per hour

$m = 5$

Utilisation of the checkout counter,

$$u = \frac{10}{(4.35 \times 5)}$$

$$= 0.46$$

Average waiting time in queue,

$$W_q = \left(\frac{1.5^2 + 3^2}{2} \right) \left(\frac{0.46^{\sqrt{2(5+1)}-1}}{5\,(1-0.46)} \right) \times 0.23$$

$$= \left(\frac{11.25}{2} \right) \left(\frac{0.46^{\sqrt{12}-1}}{5 \times 0.54} \right) \times 0.23$$

$$= (5.625) \left(\frac{0.46^{2.46}}{2.7} \right) \times 0.23$$

$$= 0.07 \text{ hours}$$

$$= 4.2 \text{ minutes}$$

Therefore, the average waiting time in the queue would be 4.2 minutes.

G/G/1 queuing system

G/G/1 represents a queuing system with normal arrival and processing times with only one server and no maximum limit to the queue. This is the simplified form of G/G/m queuing system, when $m = 1$.

$$u = \frac{r_a}{r_e} = r_a t_e$$

$$W_q = \left(\frac{c_a^2 + c_e^2}{2} \right) \left(\frac{u}{1-u} \right) t_e$$

$$WIP_q = r_a \times W_q$$

WORKED EXAMPLE

The following data are collected at an immigration counter at an international train station:

- Coefficient of variation of customer arrivals = 1
- Coefficient of variation of processing time = 3.5
- Average arrival rate of customers = 12 per hour
- Average processing rate = 16 per hour

It has been found that the customer arrival and processing time are normally distributed. We can find out the average waiting time and average number of people in the queue.

c_a = 1
c_e = 3.5
r_a = 12 per hour, therefore,
t_a = (1 / 12) hours = 5 minutes
r_e = 16 per hour, therefore,
t_e = (1 / 16) hours = 0.062 hours = 3.75 minutes

Utilisation of the single immigration counter,

$$u = \frac{12}{16} = 0.75$$

Waiting time in queue,

$$W_q = \left(\frac{1^2 + 3.5^2}{2}\right)\left(\frac{0.75}{1-0.75}\right) \times 0.062$$

$$= \left(\frac{1+12.25}{2}\right)\left(\frac{0.75}{0.25}\right) \times 0.062$$

$$= 1.24 \text{ hours}$$

$$= 74.53 \text{ minutes}$$

Average number of people in queue,

$$WIP_q = 12 \times 1.24$$

$$= 14.88$$

Therefore, the average waiting time in the queue would be 1.24 hours and the average number of people in the queue would be 14.88 i.e. approximately 15.

Questions

2.8.1 (M/M/m)

Deonte is the operations manager in a non-government organisation (NGO), providing food for people in Uganda. One of the activities of his team is to distribute the monthly quota of food in his area. With his experience Deonte learns that the arrival rate of people and the food processing rate are exponentially distributed. On average 18 people arrive every hour. There are 4 distribution counters, which on average take 7 minutes to serve a person. What would be the waiting time and number of people in the queue?

2.8.2 (M/M/m)

If the arrival rate of people has drastically increased to 30 per hour, how would it affect the waiting time and the number of people in the queue?

2.8.3 (M/M/m)
In the original problem (2.8.1), if the number of distribution counters is reduced to 3, what would be the waiting time in the queue?

2.8.4 (M/M/1)
A waitress at the service counter in a coffee shop normally takes 6 minutes to serve a customer. If customers arrive at the rate of 8 per hour and the arrival and processing times are exponentially distributed, estimate the waiting time and average number of customers in the queue.

2.8.5 (M/M/1)
If Robert wishes to reduce the waiting time in a queue from 24 minutes to 5 minutes, what would be the average processing time for each customer (assuming that the utilisation of the counter is unchanged)?

2.8.6 (M/M/1)
If the arrival rate of customers is 10 per hour, what would be the processing rate to get the service counter utilisation to the level of 0.9?

2.8.7 (G/G/m)
An airline company wishes to study the queuing system during peak hours at 4 check-in counters at Heathrow's new terminal. The following data has been collected by the operations manager:

- Passenger arrival times are normally (generally) distributed.
- Processing times at check-in counters are also normally (generally) distributed.
- Coefficient of variation of passenger arrivals is 1.5.
- Coefficient of variation of processing time is 3.5.
- Average arrival rate of passengers is 10 per hour.
- Average processing rate at check-out counter is 6 per hour.

What would be the waiting time of passengers in the queue?

2.8.8 (G/G/m)
If the coefficient of variation in processing time is reduced to 2.5, how would it affect the waiting time of passengers in the queue?

2.8.9 (G/G/m)
In the original problem (2.8.7), if the coefficient of variation in arrival time is increased from 1.5 to 2.0 and the coefficient of variation in processing time is reduced from 3.5 to 3.0, how would it affect the waiting time of passengers in the queue?

2.8.10 (G/G/1)
At a railway station ticket counter, the following information regarding the queuing system has been collected:

- Passengers' arrival times are normally distributed.
- Processing times at ticket counter are normally distributed.
- Coefficient of variation in passenger arrivals is 1.0.
- Coefficient of variation in processing time is 3.0.
- Average arrival rate of passengers is 15 per hour.
- Average processing rate at ticket counter is 20 per hour.

What would be the average number of passengers in the queue?

2.8.11 (G/G/1)
If the coefficient of variation in processing time is reduced to 1.5, how would it affect the number of passengers in the queue?

2.8.12 (G/G/1)
In the original problem 2.8.10, if the coefficient of variation in arrival time is increased from 1. 0 to 1.5 and the coefficient of variation in processing time is reduced from 3.0 to 2.5, how would it affect the number of passengers in the queue?

CHAPTER 3

Evaluative techniques

Introduction

Decision making in operations management often involves comparison between a number of alternative options so as to assess their various advantages and disadvantages. **Evaluative techniques** are those that help us carry out this process. Here we focus on the quantitative techniques, but remember that there are also many qualitative techniques. Whether qualitative or quantitative, evaluative techniques often involve looking at three aspects of any particular option:

- Feasibility – do we have the operational, management and financial capacity to do it?
- Acceptability – what benefits will the option bring us (or potentially bring us)?
- Vulnerability – what are the risks involved in adopting this option. In other words, what could go wrong and what would the consequences be?

Most of the techniques in this section are particularly helpful if assessing the acceptability of various options, but some (for example, the weighted score technique) could also be used to examine feasibility and vulnerability.

3.1 Break-even analysis

Break-even analysis can be used to identify the volume or demand necessary to achieve profitability. The objective is to find the break-even point – the point where costs equal revenues (see Figure 3.1).

Break-even analysis requires an estimation of revenue, fixed costs and variable costs. The revenue function shows by how much total revenue increases by selling additional goods or services. Fixed costs, such as depreciation, taxes, debt and rent, remain the same regardless of output. Variable costs, including materials and labour, are the proportion of total cost directly affected by output.

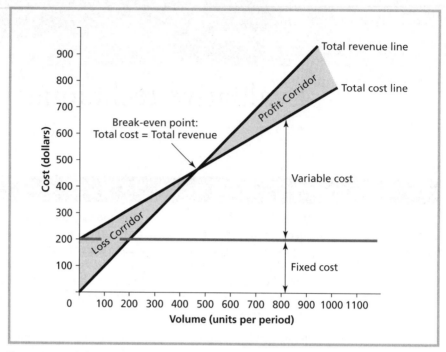

Figure 3.1 Basic break-even point. Virtually *no* variable costs are linear, but we make that assumption here.

Source: Heizer, J. and Render, B. (2006) *Operations Management*, Eighth Edition. Upper Saddle River, NJ: Pearson, Figure S7.5, p. 292.

Break-even point for a single product/service

The formulas for the break-even point in units and in cost – in this case € – are shown below:

BEP_x = break-even point in units $BEP_€$ = break-even point in euros
P = price per unit after discounts F = fixed costs
x = number of units produced V = variable costs
TR = total revenue = Px TC = total costs = $F + Vx$

The break-even point occurs when total revenue equals total costs:

$$TR = TC \quad \text{or} \quad Px = F + Vx$$

Solving for x (number of units produced) gives the following equations:

$$BEP_x = \frac{F}{P - V}$$

$$BEP_€ = BEP_x P = \frac{F}{P - V} P = \frac{F}{(P - V)/P} = \frac{F}{1 - (V/P)}$$

WORKED EXAMPLE

Alberta Inc. sells its products at €9.50 per unit. Its fixed costs are €25,000 in this period; labour costs are €2.50 per unit; and material costs are €1.25 per unit. We can calculate the break-even point in units and in euros as follows:

$$\text{Break-even in units} = \frac{F}{P-V} = \frac{25,000}{9.50-(2.50+1.25)} = 4,347.8 \text{ units}$$

$$\text{Break-even in euros} = \frac{F}{1-(V/P)} = \frac{25,000}{1-[(2.50+1.25)/(9.50)]} = \frac{25,000}{0.6053} = €41,302$$

Break-even point for multiple products/services

Most firms have a variety of offerings, each with a different price and variable cost. The break-even equation can be modified to reflect the proportion of sales for each product or service.

$$BEP_{€} = \frac{F}{\sum\left[\left(1-\frac{V_i}{P_i}\right)\times(W_i)\right]}$$

Where V = variable costs
F = fixed costs
P = price per unit after discounts
W = percent of each product/service in relation to total sales
i = each product/service

WORKED EXAMPLE

Caffé Roberto has fixed costs of €2,500 per month and sells the following four items:

Item	Price (€)	Variable cost (€)	Annual sales (units)
Latte	1.80	.60	4,500
Cappuccino	2.40	.75	5,000
Cioccolatta	3.50	1.10	2,000
Espresso	1.25	.30	7,000

We can calculate the break-even point for the following multi-product case. Before we can proceed with break-even analysis, we must weight each of the items by its proportion of total sales.

1	2	3	4	5	6	7	8
Item (i)	Price (P)	Variable cost (V)	(V/P)	1 – (V/P)	Annual revenue (€)	Proportion of sales revenue	Weighted contribution (col.5 × col.7)
Latte	1.80	.60	.33	.67	8,100	.226	.151
Cappuccino	2.40	.75	.31	.69	12,000	.335	.231
Cioccolatta	3.50	1.10	.31	.69	7,000	.195	.135
Espresso	1.25	.30	.24	.76	8,750	.244	.185
Total					35,850	1.00	.702

Worked example *continued*

For example, the revenue for lattes is €8,100 (1.80 × 4,500), which is 22.6% of the total revenue of €35,850. Therefore the contribution of lattes (€0.67) is weighted by .226 to give its contribution *relative* to the other items. Using this approach for each item, we find the total weighted contribution is .702 for each euro of sales, and the break-even point is €42,735.

$$BEP_\epsilon = \frac{F}{\sum\left[\left(1 - \frac{V_i}{P_i}\right) \times (W_i)\right]} = \frac{2{,}500 \times 12}{.702} = \frac{30{,}000}{.702} = €42{,}735$$

If we assume that Caffé Roberto operates 340 days per year, we can calculate the daily sales required to break even as follows:

$$\frac{42{,}735}{340} = €125.69$$

We can also see how many espressos must be sold each day to break even: espressos sell for €1.25 and represent 22.4% of sales revenue. Therefore the number of espressos they need to sell each day is:

$$\frac{.224 \times 125.69}{1.25} = \frac{28.15}{1.25} = 22.52 \approx 23 \text{ espressos each day.}$$

Evaluating alternative processes

Break-even analysis can also be used to assess the relative merits of two options. Rather than find the quantity at which total costs equal total revenues, here we want to find the point at which the total costs for the two alternatives are equal. If the alternatives relate to a make or buy decision, it is the quantity at which total 'make' costs equal total 'buy' costs. To find the break-even point in units (BEP_x), we set the cost functions of the two alternatives (a and b) equal and solve for x:

$$F_a + V_a x = F_b + V_b x$$

$$\text{Therefore: } x = \frac{F_a - F_b}{V_b - V_a} \text{ or if this was a make or buy decision}$$

$$x = \frac{F_m - F_b}{V_b - V_m}$$

WORKED EXAMPLE

The manager of a sandwich bar is looking to add fruit salads to the menu and expects to sell 30,000 each year. The first option (make) is to install a fruits counter with a variety of cut fruits and let the customers 'assemble' their salads. This will require the leasing of the fruit counter and additional labour to prepare the fruit, giving fixed costs of £14,500 per year and variable costs of £0.80 per salad. The second option (buy) is to sell pre-packaged salads purchased from a local supplier at £1.30 per salad, with fixed costs of £3,000 per year. We can use this information to calculate the break-even quantity:

$$\text{Break-even quantity for make or buy} = \frac{F_m - F_b}{V_b - V_m} = \frac{14{,}500 - 3{,}000}{1.30 - .80} = 23{,}000 \text{ fruit salads}$$

The break-even quantity is 23,000 salads. As sales are forecast to reach 30,000 the 'make' option is preferable. Only if the manager expected fewer than 23,000 sales would it be better to buy in pre-packaged fruit salads.

Questions

3.1.1 Perfection Ltd sells bottles of shampoo at £5.95 each. The firm has variable costs totaling £2.50 per unit and fixed costs of £3,250 per month. How many bottles will the company have to sell to break even?

3.1.2 Perfection Ltd decides to invest in new machinery which brings their variable cost down to £1.25 per unit, but their fixed costs rise to £4,200 per month. What is the new break-even point and sales revenue?

3.1.3 BETA private hospital offers a facelift operation for £2,450. The fixed costs related to this service are £750,000 and the variable cost for each procedure is £975. What is the break-even point in sales revenue for the operation?

3.1.4 Dreams Inc. is a small company selling wedding cakes in southern Spain. The firm's fixed costs total €265,000 per year, their labour costs are €30 per cake and materials cost €22 per cake. Ricardo Ramos, the marketing manager, expects to sell 3,000 cakes each year and wants the average price to be €120. Will the firm break even with this strategy?

3.1.5 Would it be better for Dreams Inc. to reduce their fixed costs from €265,000 to €175,000 or to reduce their labour costs from €30 to €15?

3.1.6 The table below sets out the 6 key products sold at Lucca's Pizza Palace. Given an annual fixed cost of €17,000, what is the break-even annual sales revenue for the company?

Item	Price (€)	Variable cost (€)	Annual sales (pizzas)
Margherita	6.00	2.00	7,500
Napoli	7.50	2.50	5,000
Americano	7.50	2.75	6,500
Quattro Formaggi	8.50	3.00	8,500
Tropicano	8.00	3.00	4,000
Funghi	7.00	2.25	6,500

3.1.7 Lucca's Pizza Palace is currently open for business 250 nights per year. What are the daily sales required to break even?

3.1.8 What is the average daily profit made by Lucca's Pizza Palace?

3.1.9 Axon Synthetics is considering the relative merits of two fabric dye machines. Machine *a* will have a fixed cost of $245,000 and a per garment variable cost of $3.50. Machine *b* has a fixed cost of $135,000, but costs $4.15 for each garment. At what quantity does machine *a* look to be a better investment?

3.1.10 If Axon is able to buy machine *a* for $200,000 and the variable cost per garment for machine *b* rises from $4.15 to $4.35, what is the effect on the break-even point for the two options?

3.1.11 Axon has now been approached by another firm which wants Axon to invest in its most up-to-date dyeing machine (*c*). This will cost the firm $450,000 in fixed costs, but the variable cost will be drastically reduced to just $1.65 per garment. Axon is expecting demand over the year to be 240,000 garments. Should it invest in machine *c*? Note the fixed costs for machine *a* are now $200,000. What are the total costs for the two options if demand forecasts are met?

3.2 Weighted score method

Decisions often don't rely on a single measure, such as cost. The **weighted-score method** (also called a **preference matrix** or the **factor-rating method**) is a useful technique for comparing two or more alternatives which have multiple criteria. It is particularly useful when alternatives have costs that are hard to evaluate, such as location decisions, product development options or technology acquisitions. The technique involves allocating scores for the factors that are significant in the decision and weighting each score by the significance of the factor. Scores can be on any scale, but the sum of weights for all factors typically equals 1.0 or 100. The total score for each alternative is the sum of weighted scores.

WORKED EXAMPLE

Centro Parc, a chain of activity-based hotels in Europe, is considering two possible sites for expansion – Barcelona, Spain, and Marseille, France. The rating sheet below lists the critical success factor, with their weighting, as determined by Centro's management.

Critical success factors	Weight	Scores (out of 100)	
		Barcelona	Marseille
Labour skills	.30	65	70
Access to market	.20	80	65
Per capita income	.10	50	60
Tax structure	.25	45	30
Potential for expansion	.15	60	90
Totals	**1.00**		

We can use this information to determine the site that appears to be the best for development:

Critical success factors	Weight	Weighted score (score × weight)	
		Barcelona	Marseille
Labour skills	.30	19.5	21
Access to market	.20	16	13
Per capita income	.10	5	6
Tax structure	.25	11.25	7.5
Potential for expansion	.15	9	13.5
Totals	**1.00**	**60.75**	**61.0**

The Marseille site marginally outperforms the Barcelona site based on the weighted score method. It also has the advantage of performing better on the most important success factor identified by management – labour skills.

Questions 3.2.1 Vladin Bank, based in Moscow, is considering investing in two new banking services – upgraded online accounts and personal banking for high earners. It can only afford to invest in one of these options. Based on the ratings sheet below, what would you recommend?

		Scores (out of 100)	
Critical success factors	Weight	Upgrade online accounts	Personal banking
Market potential	.35	85	75
Labour skills	.15	80	50
Unit profit margin	.10	60	90
Operations capability	.10	60	75
Risk	.15	70	75
Investment required	.15	40	60
Totals	**1.00**		

3.2.2 The following table shows the performance criteria, weights and scores (1–9) for a potential new microchip. The operations manager only wants to introduce one product during the year and so far the highest total for any other product idea is 7.35. Should the firm invest in the new microchip?

Performance criteria	Weight	Scores (1–9)
Market potential	.25	5
Competitive advantage	.10	7
Unit profit margin	.30	8
Location of supply	.05	3
Risk	.10	5
Investment required	.20	5
Total	**1.00**	

3.2.3 Bryson Promotions, located in Wellington, New Zealand, is screening three new service ideas. Resource constraints allow for only one of them to be commercialised. Each factor has been given an equal weighting of 0.20. Based on the table below, which product should the firm invest in?

	Scores (out of 100)		
Critical success factors	Service A	Service B	Service C
Demand uncertainty	60	70	40
Expected ROI	75	50	90
Unit profit margin	35	75	80
Operations capability	60	45	30
Compatibility with current service	50	45	35

3.2.4 A water park is considering two locations for development – one in France and one in Spain. Based on the following weightings for the factors below, which country represents the best location?

Factor description	Weight	France	Spain
Proximity to market	.30	80	50
Infrastructure	.20	50	40
Weather	.25	30	70
Labour availability	.25	60	80

3.3 Decision theory

Decision theory is an approach that is useful when outcomes are associated with uncertain alternatives. It is popular in areas such as process, capacity, location and inventory, where decisions relate to an uncertain future. With decision theory, managers make choices using the following steps:

1 List the feasible alternatives.
2 List the events (also called chance events or states of nature) that have an impact on the outcome of the choice but are under the firm's control.
3 Calculate a payoff table, which shows the amount for each alternative event.
4 Estimate the likelihood of each event, using past experience, expert opinion or forecasting, making sure probabilities sum to 1.0.
5 Select a decision rule to evaluate the alternatives, such as lowest expected cost.

Using this 5-step approach, we examine decisions under three different situations – certainty, uncertainty and risk.

Decision making under certain conditions

In an ideal world, an operations manager will know which event will occur and can select the alternative with the best payoff. For example, a firm is deciding whether to build a small or large customer services office to deal with queries, orders and complaints. A lot depends on how high or low future demand turns out to be. The firm know with certainty the payoff that will result under each alternative, shown in the following payoff table (in £000 at present values of future profits).

	Possible future demand	
Alternative	Low	High
Small office	260	350
Large office	210	1050
Do nothing	0	0

If the firm knows that future demand will be low, they should invest in a small office because it gives a payoff of £260,000 compared with £210,000 for a large office and £0 if they do nothing. However, if they are sure demand will be high, they should clearly invest in a large office and enjoy the higher payoff (£1,050,000 compared with £350,000).

WORKED EXAMPLE

In reality, it is unlikely that a firm can be so confident about future demand! In which case, operations managers can follow four different decision rules to determine the best course of action:

1 **Maximin.** The pessimist anticipates the 'worst' event and selects the best alternative for this scenario.
2 **Maximax.** The optimist anticipates the 'best' event and selects the best alternative for this scenario.

Worked example *continued*

3 **Laplace**. The realist assumes all events are equally likely. If there are n events, this rule assumes the probability of each event is $1/n$. The payoff of each alternative is then weighted based on these probabilities.

4 **Minimax regret**. Choose the alternative with the best 'worst regret'. Calculate a table of regrets (opportunity losses). A 'regret' is the difference between a given payoff and the best payoff in the column. For an event, it shows how much is lost by picking an alternative to the best option for an event.

Reconsider the payoff matrix for the firm considering alternative customer service options. We can see the decision that management should take following the four different decision rules:

(a) *Maximin*. The worst payoff for each alternative is the *lowest* number in its row of the payoff matrix. In this case the worst case scenarios are £260,000 for the small office and £210,000 for a large office. Therefore, under this rule, the firm would invest in the small office, as it represents the best of the worst numbers.

	Possible future demand	
Alternative	Low	High
Small office	**260**	350
Large office	**210**	1,050
Do nothing	**0**	0

(b) *Maximax*. The best payoff for each alternative is the *highest* number in its row of the payoff matrix. In this case the best case scenarios are £350,000 for the small office and £1,050,000 for a large office. Therefore, under this rule, the firm would invest in the large office, as it represents the best of the best numbers.

	Possible future demand	
Alternative	Low	High
Small office	260	**350**
Large office	210	**1,050**
Do nothing	0	**0**

(c) *Laplace*. Using this rule we assign equal probability to all events – in this case 0.5. The weighted payoffs are therefore £305,000 for the small office and £630,000 for a large office. Therefore, under this rule, the firm would invest in the large office, as it represents the best of the weighted numbers.

	Possible future demand	
Alternative	Low	High
Small office	**0.5 × 260**	**0.5 × 350**
Large office	**0.5 × 210**	**0.5 × 1050**
Do nothing	**0.5 × 0**	**0.5 × 0**

(d) *Minimax regret*. If demand turns out to be low, the best alternative is the small office, as its regret is zero. If a large office is built and demand is low, regret would be 50 (260 – 210). However, if demand is high and only a small office is built, regret is 700 (1,050 – 350). Under the *minimax regret* rule we look to avoid maximum regret, so invest in the large office.

	Regret	
Alternative	Low	High
Small office	260 – 260 = 0	**1,050 – 350 = 700**
Large office	260 – 210 = 50	1,050 – 1,050 = 0

Decision making under uncertain conditions

Whilst it is indeed rare to have certain forecast demand, in many cases a manager is able to estimate the probabilities of different events occurring. In this case, we can use a weighting system, called the **expected value** decision rule. This is like the *Laplace* decision rule, except the events are no longer assumed to be equally probable.

WORKED EXAMPLE

If we consider the office investment worked example, let us assume that the likelihood of high future demand is just 5% (0.05) instead of 50% assumed under uncertainty decision rules. Using the expected value decision rule, we see a weighted payoff of £264.50 for the small office and £252.00 for the large office. The effect of changing the probability is to change the decision from the large office investment to the small office investment.

	Probable future demand	
Alternative	Low (.95)	High .05)
Small office	0.95 × 260	0.05 × 350
Large office	0.95 × 210	0.05 × 1,050
Do nothing	0.95 × 0	0.05 × 0

The value of perfect information

The value of perfect information is determined by the amount an expected payoff would improve if future events are certain instead of uncertain. It can be found by:

1 identifying the best payoff for each event
2 calculating the expected value of these best payoffs by multiplying them by the probability of events occurring
3 subtracting the expected value of the payoff without perfect information from the expected value with perfect information. The difference is the value of perfect information.

WORKED EXAMPLE

Using the payoff matrix below, calculate the value of perfect information if the probability of low demand is 0.4 and high demand is 0.6.

	Future demand & profits (€)	
Alternative	Low (0.4)	High (0.6)
Small machine	€20,000	€32,000
Large machine	€15,000	€52,000
Do nothing	0	0

The best payoff for each event is the highest number in each matrix column – €20,000 for low

demand, €52,000 for high demand. The best expected value (*EV*) without perfect information is for the large machine, whereas for perfect information we have both best payoffs:

$$EV_{imperfect} = (0.4 \times 15,000) + (0.6 \times 52,000)$$
$$= €37,200$$

$$EV_{perfect} = (0.4 \times 20,000) + (0.6 \times 52,000)$$
$$= €39,200$$

Therefore, the value of perfect information is €39,200 – €37,200 = €2,000. A manager should not pay more than this to gain a perfect forecast.

Questions

3.3.1 Stephanie Dunitz, the CEO of Avitar Publishing, is considering whether to order 50,000 books or 100,000 for a new novel due for release. She knows the payoff that will result under each alternative, shown in the following payoff table (in €000 at present values of future profits).

	Possible future demand	
Alternative	40,000 sales	90,000 sales
50,000 books	180	210
100,000 books	110	550
Do nothing	0	0

Stephanie is unsure what future demand will be. What decision should she make following the *maximin*, *maximax*, *laplace* and *minimax regret* decision-making criteria for uncertainty?

3.3.2 Stephanie has now received market data to suggest that there is a 65% chance that no more than 40,000 books will be sold. Using the *expected value* decision-making criteria, what should she do?

3.3.3 Given the .65 and .35 respectively for low and high sales of the book, what is the value of perfect information?

3.3.4 Graham Alexander manages a chocolate shop in Bath, England and is purchasing special 'love' chocolates from a supplier on the Isle of Skye, in Scotland. Given how small advance sales are for Valentine's Day, Graham has no way of knowing for sure whether his sales will be low (50 boxes), medium (100 boxes) or high (200 boxes). He pays £8 per box and sells them for £25. Assuming any unsold chocolates cannot be sold, construct a payoff table and identify what decisions Graham would take under the following decision criteria:

(a) *maximin*
(b) *maximax*
(c) *laplace*
(d) *minimax regret*.

3.3.5 Reconsider the example of the chocolate shop. The following year, Graham is considering how many boxes of special chocolates to order. The options and profits are the same, but this year he has more of an idea of likely sales. There is a 30% chance of 50 boxes selling, 50% chance of 100 boxes selling and 20% chance of 200 boxes selling. What effect does this have on Graham's decision if he uses either the *maximax* or the *expected value* (*weighted laplace*) criteria?

3.3.6 Alixar Defence Solutions (ADS) is considering three small products, code-named Alpha 1, Delta 4 and Gamma 7. The demand for products will vary depending on the outcome of a spending review by the Ministry of Defence. The tables below show the expected demand for the three products, their costs and price.

	Possible future defence strategies & impact on demand		
Alternative	'Micro Engagement'	'Euro-Collaboration'	'Turbo Thrust'
Alpha 1	10,000	5,000	20,000
Delta 4	5,000	15,000	30,000
Gamma 7	15,000	25,000	10,000
Do nothing	0	0	0

	Product		
Alternative	Alpha 1	Delta 4	Gamma 7
Fixed costs	£450,000	£500,000	£800,000
Variable cost per unit	£60	£150	£250
Price per unit	£200	£350	£500

Construct a payoff table for this situation and identify what decisions ADS should take under the following decision criteria:

(a) *maximin*
(b) *maximax*
(c) *laplace*.

3.3.7 Consider the case of Alixar Defence Solutions (ADS). If the probabilities of the three different scenarios are now not considered equal, but instead as follows, what is the effect on the decision using the *expected value* decision-making criteria?

- Probability of Micro Engagement = 0.4
- Probability of Euro-Collaboration = 0.2
- Probability of Turbo Thrust = 0.4

3.4 Decision trees

Decision trees are often used by operations managers when decisions result in outcomes which in turn require further decisions and have further outcomes. The objective of these trees is to determine the **expected monetary value (EMV)** of each course of action. The technique can be used in a wide range of operations areas, such as considering the merits of alternative product design options, technology or capacity investments, and even staff training programmes.

WORKED EXAMPLE

Zetec Inc. is considering its options for a new handheld drill. The first option is to purchase an advanced CAD system; the second is to employ several new design engineers to work on the project; and the third is not to develop the drill at all. The cost of purchasing the CAD system is €950,000, whilst hiring additional design engineers is €725,000. When manufacturing without CAD, unit costs are €100, but when using CAD they fall to €80. If the new product is favourably received by the market, it is expected that 50,000 units will be sold at €200 each. However, there is a 60% chance that the product will be less successful, in which case only 16,000 units are expected to be sold. We can now calculate the expected monetary values (EMVs) for the three options:

Worked example *continued*

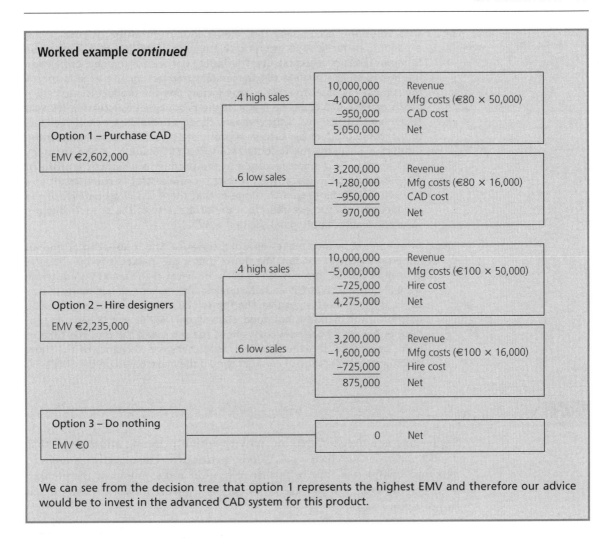

We can see from the decision tree that option 1 represents the highest EMV and therefore our advice would be to invest in the advanced CAD system for this product.

3.4.1 The product's expected life-cycle sales are 150,000 units, costing £75 to produce and selling for £150. Machine A will cost £365,000, with a .80 probability of yielding 87 good parts per 100 and a .20 probability of yielding 92 good parts per 100. Machine B costs £400,000 with a .75 probability of yielding 92 good parts per 100 and a .25 probability of yielding 87 good parts per 100. Calculate the EMV for the two machine options.

3.4.2 Jean-Paul, the CEO of Dupreti Inc., has the option of (a) proceeding with the production of a new flat screen television that has completed pilot testing, or (b) getting a team to undertake a market research study before releasing the product. If Jean-Paul decides to go straight into production, the TVs will retail at €550. The company believes there is a .6 probability of 100,000 units selling and a .4 probability of 75,000 units selling. However, if he decides to wait until further market research has been carried out, the TVs will sell at €750, with a .7 probability of 75,000 and a .3 probability of 70,000 units selling. The cost of market research is €100,000. Which option has the higher expected monetary value (EMV)?

3.4.3 Sofa Solutions, a company that makes lounge furniture, is considering expanding its facilities to incorporate a new sofa design which is yet to be tested in terms of marketability. The facility options for the new production line are: to build a small factory, a medium-sized factory or a large factory. If the company chooses to build a large factory and the product is a success, a profit of £150,000 could be made. If the product is unsuccessful, it could result in a £120,000 loss. If the company chooses to build a medium-sized factory and the product is a success, a profit of £90,000 could be made. If the product is unsuccessful, it could result in a £65,000 loss. If the company chooses to build a small factory and the product is a success, a profit of £50,000 could be made. If the product is unsuccessful, it could result in a £10,000 loss. Recent research suggests that there is a .6 probability of the product being a success, therefore the probability of the product being a failure is .4. Which option has the best EMV?

3.4.4 Jacqueline Mulvaney makes bespoke corsages. She is about to attend an important show in London. She thinks that if the market is favourable, she can sell 50 deluxe corsages at £75 each. However, if the market is not good, she will only sell 35 at £65 each. Jacqueline also makes a simple-range of corsages. If the market is positive, she can sell 80 simple corsages at £45 each, whereas if the market is not good, she will only sell 60 at £38 each. To produce either set of corsages costs about the same and she only has time to make one range. If Jacqueline feels that there is a .5 chance of the show going well, which range of corsages should she make based on the EMV?

3.5 Sequencing

Sequencing is a decision-making activity within planning and control that decides the order in which work is to be performed. The objective is often to maximise completion time or facility utilisation and to minimise the number of jobs in the system or average lateness. The sequence of work is determined by pre-defined rules.

Sequencing rules

Some of the most popular sequencing rules are detailed below.

UK term	US term
Priority	
DD (due date)	**EDD** (earliest due date)
FIFO (first in first out)	**FCFS** (first come first served)
LIFO (last in first out)	**LCFS** (last come first served)
LOT (longest operation time)	**LPT** (longest processing time)
SOT (shortest operation time)	**SPT** (shortest processing time)

WORKED EXAMPLE

Xao Ling is an events coordinator for a small company in the Anhui province in China. Returning from her annual holiday, she is given six events to plan. She gives them the codes A–F. She needs to decide upon the sequence in which to plan the events and wants to minimise the average time the jobs are tied up in the office and, if possible, meet the deadlines allocated.

She first considers using **FIFO**:

Sequence of jobs	Process time (days)	Start time	Finish time	Due date	Lateness (days)
A	4	0	4	12	0
B	3	4	7	5	2
C	1	7	8	7	1
D	2	8	10	9	1
E	2	10	12	15	0
F	5	12	17	8	9
		Total time in process = 58 days Average time in process = total/6 = 9.67 days		Total lateness = 13 days Average lateness = total/6 = 2.17 days	

She wonders if she can do any better, so she tries the **DD** rule:

Sequence of jobs	Process time (days)	Start time	Finish time	Due date	Lateness (days)
B	3	0	3	5	0
C	1	3	4	7	0
F	5	4	9	8	1
D	2	9	11	9	2
A	4	11	15	12	3
E	2	15	17	15	2
		Total time in process = 59 days Average time in process = total/6 = 9.83 days		Total lateness = 8 days Average lateness = total/6 = 1.33 days	

Jane then tries out the **SOT** rule:

Sequence of jobs	Process time (days)	Start time	Finish time	Due date	Lateness (days)
C	1	0	1	7	0
D	2	1	3	9	0
E	2	3	5	15	0
B	3	5	8	5	3
A	4	8	12	12	0
F	5	12	17	8	9
		Total time in process = 46 days Average time in process = total/6 = 7.67 days		Total lateness = 12 days Average lateness = total/6 = 2 days	

If her efficiency is most important to her, she would use the **SOT** rule. If lateness is most important to her, she would use the **DD** rule.

Critical ratio

An alternative sequencing rule is the **critical ratio (CR)**. This rule often performs better than other rules such as **DD, FIFO, LIFO, SOT**, and **LOT**. The priority of jobs using the **CR** rule is defined by an index computed as follows:

$$CR = \frac{Time\ remaining}{Workdays\ remaining} = \frac{Due\ date - Today's\ date}{Workdays\ remaining}$$

WORKED EXAMPLE

Today is day 55 on J. Ashby Architect's schedule. We can compute the critical ratios for the 4 design jobs outstanding as follows:

Job	Due date	Workdays remaining	CR
A	60	2.0	(60 – 55)/2 = 2.500
B	68	5.0	(68 – 55)/5 = 2.600
C	71	3.0	(71 – 55)/3 = 5.333
D	72	8.0	(72 – 55)/8 = 2.125

Therefore, the priority of jobs using the **CR** rule is D, A, B, C. Once job D is complete, we would re-calculate the critical ratios for the remaining jobs to determine if their priorities have changed.

Johnson's rule – sequencing for 2-station flow

The next level of complexity in sequencing is when a job goes through two different machines or servers in the same order. In this case, **Johnson's rule** can be used to minimise the processing time of jobs. This involves a four-step process:

1 All jobs are listed with required processing time for each machine.
2 The shortest job time is selected. If it is with the first machine, the job is scheduled first. If it is with the second machine, the job is scheduled last.
3 Once a job is scheduled, it is eliminated.
4 Steps 2 and 3 are repeated until all jobs have been sequenced.

WORKED EXAMPLE

A gardener has a number of jobs which require two steps – clearance and planting. The time for processing each job is as follows:

Job	Clearance (hrs)	Planting (hrs)
A	8	3 (7th)
B	4 (2nd)	6
C	11	8 (5th)
D	14	7 (6th)
E	2 (1st)	2
F	5 (3rd)	8
G	6 (4th)	9

In this case, the shortest processing time is 2 hours for job E. Because this is at the first process (clearance), job E is assigned first position in the schedule. The next shortest processing time is 3 hours for job A. Because this is at the second process (planting), job A is sequenced last. We continue this process until all jobs have been sequenced. The final sequence is E, B, F, G, C, D, A.

3.5.1 It is day 6 in a job schedule. The processing time and due dates of four jobs are shown below. Using the **SOT** rule, in what order should the jobs be processed?

Job	Processing time (days)	Job due date (days)
A	23	30
B	45	28
C	20	40
D	13	10

3.5.2 Jackie is a trainee reporter. On Monday 7 November, she arrives at work, pleased that she cleared all of her work on Friday. She finds five new jobs to be completed and decides to start straight away:

Job	Required processing time	Due date
A	3 days	14 November
B	1 day	10 November
C	9 days	21 November
D	4 days	11 November
E	6 days	17 November

Jackie only works from *Monday to Friday*.

(a) Using the first-in first-out rule, calculate the total time in process, total lateness, average time in process and average lateness.

(b) Using the due date rule, calculate the total time in process, total lateness, average time in process and average lateness.

(c) Using the shortest operation time rule, calculate the total time in process, total lateness, average time in process and average lateness.

(d) Which rule should Jackie adopt if the most important factor is the average time in process?

3.5.3 Thomas is a wooden-toy maker. After a summer holiday with his family, he returns home to Cornwall to find five orders in the post:

Job	Required processing time	Due date (number of days)
A	5 days	7
B	12 days	14
C	2 days	10
D	19 days	20
E	8 days	8

(a) Using the first-in first-out rule, calculate the total time in process, total lateness, average time in process and average lateness.

(b) Using the due date rule, calculate the total time in process, total lateness, average time in process and average lateness.

(c) Using the shortest operation time rule, calculate the total time in process, total lateness, average time in process and average lateness.

(d) Which rule should Thomas adopt if he is most concerned with lateness?

3.5.4 Today is day 20 on the work schedule for four data analysis jobs in a financial services firm. What are the critical ratios and priority of the jobs?

Job	Due date	Workdays remaining
A	24	2
B	28	11
C	30	7
D	38	8

3.5.5 It is day 14 on the work schedule for an accounting firm based in New York, USA. What are the critical ratios and priority of the jobs remaining?

Job	Due date	Workdays remaining	CR
A	15	2.0	0.500
B	17	2.5	1.200
C	18	9.0	0.444
D	20	4.0	1.500
E	38	7.0	3.429
F	35	4.0	5.250

3.5.6 A card-maker has four large orders for celebration cards which require two steps – cutting and gluing. The time for processing each job is as follows:

Job	Cutting (min)	Gluing (min)
A	90	50
B	30	20
C	40	30
D	20	10

Using Johnson's rule, what is the sequence of jobs?

3.5.7 An accountant has a number of orders which require two steps. The time for processing each job is as follows:

Job	Step 1 (hrs)	Step 2 (hrs)
A	2	6
B	3	1
C	7	8
D	5	4
E	5	9
F	8	6

Using Johnson's rule, what is the sequence of jobs?

3.5.8 Use Johnson's rule to find the best sequence of processing the following jobs through the two servers.

Job	Server 1 (min)	Server 2 (min)
A	65	120
B	35	85
C	120	90
D	180	95
E	140	80
F	50	45

CHAPTER **4**

Optimising techniques

Introduction

Some techniques take the idea of evaluation further by trying to identify the very best option, that is, the one that brings the maximum net benefit to the operation. This is called **optimisation** and usually involves maximising some function such as revenue or profit or return on assets, or minimising a function such as cost or cash flow.

Optimising techniques often have three elements:

- an **objective function** which we want to minimise or maximise
- a number of **variables** which determine the value of the objective function (usually these are the things about which the technique is trying to decide)
- a number of **constraints** that allow the variables to take on certain values but exclude others.

In these terms, the purpose of an optimisation technique is to find values of the variables that minimise or maximise the objective function while satisfying the constraints.

Of course, optimisation will depend on the scope of how any problem is framed. So, for example, we might be able to optimise the amount of stock that we order at any point in time (that is, we choose the reordering level that minimises total costs of stock holding), but this may not mean that it is the best solution for the operation overall. It may be that in optimising the stock decision we are seriously disadvantaging other parts of the operation. This issue is known as the difference between local optimisation and global optimisation. Clearly, global optimisation is a significantly more difficult problem to solve given that, as the scope of the problem expands, more inter-related decisions (and therefore objective functions) are brought together in a complex whole.

4.1 Optimising location

Deciding the physical location of operations or the processes within them is challenging and expensive. There are a number of techniques that operations managers can use to optimise location, including **load-distance** and the **centre of gravity** method.

Load-distance method

The **load-distance** method is a mathematical model that selects a location based on minimising its load-distance (*ld*) score, generally by choosing a location where large loads travel short distances. The load (*l*) may be shipments to customers, from suppliers, or between facilities, or even customers travelling to the location. The distance (*d*) between two points can be measured in a variety of ways. Popular methods are as a straight line (**Euclidean distance**), as a series of 90-degree turns, as along city blocks (**Rectilinear distance**), or in time.

$$\text{Euclidean distance } D_{AB} = \sqrt{(x_A - x_B)^2 + (y_A - y_B)^2}$$

$$\text{Rectilinear distance } D_{AB} = |x_A - x_B| + |y_A - y_B|$$

$$
\begin{aligned}
\text{Where } D_{AB} &= \text{Distance between points A and B} \\
x_A &= x \text{ coordinate of point A} \\
x_B &= x \text{ coordinate of point B} \\
y_A &= y \text{ coordinate of point A} \\
y_B &= y \text{ coordinate of point B}
\end{aligned}
$$

The two measures give different results. Therefore, the key when comparing alternative locations is to be consistent in the use of one distance measure.

WORKED EXAMPLE

An Indian supermarket chain is using the load-distance method to determine where to locate a new store. It is considering two towns (B and C) with the highest expected demand (*l*). Based on the coordinates of these two locations and the coordinates of other locations which will also place demand on the new store, we can calculate the load-distances for the two options (using a rectilinear distance) as follows:

Location	x-coordinate	y-coordinate	load (000s)	Option 1 (B) distance (x)	Option 1 (B) ld	Option 2 (C) distance (x)	Option 2 (C) ld
A	2.0	4.0	3	(2 + 2) = 4	12	(6 + 2) = 8	24
B	4.0	6.0	10	(0 + 0) = 0	0	(4 + 4) = 8	80
C	8.0	2.0	8	(4 + 4) = 8	64	(0 + 0) = 0	0
D	6.0	7.0	7	(2 + 1) = 3	21	(2 + 5) = 7	49
E	6.0	4.0	5	(2 + 2) = 4	20	(2 + 2) = 4	20
					117		**173**

Based on the load-distance method, it is clearly better to locate in town B, because it has a lower *ld* score (117) than town C (173).

Load-distance for layout decisions

When assessing the relative merits of alternative layout plans within operations we can use the load-distance method in exactly the same way. In this case, the load (*l*) could be defined as the number of trips between processes and the distance between them is calculated from the plan being evaluated.

WORKED EXAMPLE

Currently, an operation has a layout based on block plan A and is considering changing to a new block plan B.

Based on the load-distance method, we can see that the new layout proposed would reduce the load-distance from 560 to 350.

Current block plan (A)			Proposed block plan (B)		
1	3	2	6	3	4
4	5	6	2	1	5

		Current plan		Proposed plan	
Process pair	Trips between processes (l)	Distance (d)	ld	Distance (d)	ld
1,2	40	2.0	80.0	1.0	40.0
1,3	30	1.0	30.0	1.0	30.0
1,5	90	2.0	180.0	1.0	90.0
2,3	15	1.0	15.0	2.0	30.0
2,4	10	3.0	30.0	3.0	30.0
3,4	75	2.0	150.0	1.0	75.0
3,6	20	2.0	40.0	1.0	20.0
4,5	35	1.0	35.0	1.0	35.0
			560.0		**350.0**

Centre of gravity method

The **centre of gravity** method is another technique used to find a location which minimises transportation costs. The coordinates of the optimum location are given as:

$$\bar{x} = \frac{\sum x_i v_i}{\sum v_i} \text{ and } \bar{y} = \frac{\sum y_i v_i}{\sum v_i}$$

Where x_i = the x coordinate of destination i
y_i = the y coordinate of destination i
v_i = the amount to be shipped to or from destination i

WORKED EXAMPLE

A national distribution centre for drinks delivers to five regional centres. Each regional centre emails its orders to the national centre when replenishment stock is required, so large stocks are not kept at the regional centres. The location and weekly loads requirement of each of the regional centres are as follows:

	x-coordinate	y-coordinate	Weekly demand
A	2	4	6 loads
B	4	7	11 loads
C	5	4	9 loads
D	8	11	15 loads
E	10	9	12 loads

Worked example *continued*

The centre-of-gravity coordinates of the lowest-cost location for the national distribution centre are calculated as follows:

$$\bar{x} = \frac{\sum x_i v_i}{\sum v_i} = \frac{(2 \times 6) + (4 \times 11) + (5 \times 9) + (8 \times 15) + (10 \times 12)}{53} = 6.43$$

$$\bar{y} = \frac{\sum y_i v_i}{\sum v_i} = \frac{(4 \times 6) + (7 \times 11) + (4 \times 9) + (11 \times 15) + (9 \times 12)}{53} = 7.74$$

Questions

4.1.1 A window cleaner is considering locating his premises in either Alton or Brackley. He estimates his yearly demand for these and other surrounding villages in hundreds per annum. Using the rectilinear distance, what are the load-distance scores for the two options?

				Alton	Brackley
Location	x-coordinate	y-coordinate	Load (00s)	Distance (x)	Distance (x)
Alton	3.0	4.0	20	0.0	5.0
Brackley	5.0	7.0	25	5.0	0.0
Cowley	5.0	3.0	18	3.0	4.0
Deston	6.0	7.0	8	6.0	1.0
Easton	8.0	2.0	4	7.0	8.0
Faxted	4.0	4.0	12	1.0	4.0

4.1.2 Which location should be chosen if the demand from Deston falls to 500 and increases in Faxted to 1800?

4.1.3 A piano tuner has a choice of locating either in Bristol or Tetbury. Based on the weekly hours of demand and times to drive to other locations, use the load-distance method to calculate the best location.

		Bristol	Tetbury
Location	Weekly hours (l)	Time (mins)	Time (mins)
Bath	12	40.0	30.0
Bristol	10	0.0	60.0
Frome	7	120.0	160.0
Tetbury	4	60.0	0.0
Cheltenham	9	90.0	30.0

4.1.4 The piano tuner also has the option of locating in Frome. Assuming the following travel times, would this result in a lower *ld* score?

	Frome
Location	Time (mins)
Bath	40.0
Bristol	120.0
Frome	0.0
Tetbury	160.0
Cheltenham	190.0

4.1.5 A tool-finishing plant in Ohio is considering changing its layout and wants to see if this will reduce total load-distance. Based on the information below, calculate the load-distances for the current and proposed plans.

Current block plan			Proposed block plan		
1	2	3	1	3	6
6	5	4	4	5	2

Process pair	Trips between processes (l)
1,3	20
2,3	10
3,4	20
3,5	30
3,6	35
5,2	10
2,6	20

4.1.6 A service centre dealing with orders for kitchenware is considering a change to its current layout. Based on the information below, what is the impact on load-distance score from changing to the proposed block plan?

Current block plan			Proposed block plan		
1	2	3	1	2	9
6	5	6	6	8	3
7	8	9	5	7	4

Process pair	Trips between processes (l)
1,2	100
1,6	30
6,2	30
2,3	30
2,5	20
2,9	50
9,3	50
5,3	20
3,4	100
4,7	100
7,8	100

4.1.7 A university in Lisbon, Portugal is relocating its internal mail distribution centre. Use the following delivery and walking time information to determine the *ld* score for each location.

Location	Deliveries per week	Room 502	Room 360
Science	30	5.5 mins	8.0 mins
Social Sciences	42	7.0 mins	8.0 mins
Management	28	4.5 mins	6.0 mins
Medicine	20	9.0 mins	3.5 mins

4.1.8 A cotton supplier for four large clothes manufacturers in India is hoping to relocate. The location of each of the clothes manufacturers is as follows:

	x-coordinate	y-coordinate	Weekly demand (hrs)
A	8	5	12
B	17	22	9
C	29	16	17
D	42	30	14

Using the centre of gravity method, what coordinates would be the best location?

4.1.9 Alessandra, a cleaner living near Ravenna, Italy, is thinking about moving house and she wonders where would be the most cost effective place to live, based on the average demand from villages in the area.

	x-coordinate	y-coordinate	Weekly demand
A	3	3	8
B	5	6	4
C	7	4	9
D	8	6	12
E	10	2	6
F	12	8	5

Using the centre of gravity method, what coordinates would be Alessandra's best location?

4.1.10 What are the new low-cost coordinates for Alessandra if demand in location B increases to 16 and in location F to 6?

4.1.11 A wind turbine company is setting up a factory and, given the nature of the product, wants to find the best location to minimise transportation costs.

(a) Calculate the centre of gravity coordinates for the factory to two decimal places.
(b) Calculate the load-distance score for this location, using rectilinear distance.

Location	x-coordinate	y-coordinate	Load
A	6.0	3.0	43.0
B	5.0	4.0	67.0
C	3.0	9.0	82.0
D	4.0	6.0	33.0
E	2.0	10.0	52.0

4.2 Optimising inventory

Given the annual holding cost of inventory is typically between 20 and 40 percent of its value, there is clearly a pressure to maintain low levels of inventory. However, the risk of stock-outs, ordering costs, set-up costs, labour and equipment utilisation, transportation costs and quantity discounts all create pressure towards higher inventories. Therefore, operations managers must find a balance between the various pressures on inventory levels. There are a number of techniques for estimating inventory levels, determining how much to order (**the volume decision**) and deciding when to place orders (**the timing decision**).

Estimating inventory levels

Cycle inventory is the portion of total inventory that varies with lot size. The longer the time between orders for a given item, the higher cycle inventory will be. When an order has just been received, cycle inventory is at its maximum – Q. By the end of the interval, just before the next order arrives, cycle inventory has dropped to 0. Therefore, average cycle inventory is calculated as:

$$\text{Average cycle inventory} = \frac{Q+0}{2} = \frac{Q}{2}$$

Pipeline inventory exists because material cannot be transported instantaneously from the point of supply to the point of demand. As such, it consists of orders that have been placed, but not yet received.

$$\text{Pipeline inventory} = dL$$

Where d = average demand for an item per period

L = number of periods in the item's lead time

WORKED EXAMPLE

A supplier makes monthly shipments to 'House & Garden', in average lot sizes of 200 coffee tables. The average demand for these items is 50 tables per week, and the lead time from the supplier 3 weeks. 'House & Garden' must pay for inventory from the moment the supplier ships the products. If they are willing to increase their lot size to 300 units, the supplier will offer a lead time of 1 week. We can use this information to calculate the effect on cycle and pipeline inventories:

Current cycle inventory $= \dfrac{Q}{2} = \dfrac{200}{2} = 100$ tables

Current pipeline inventory $= dL = (50 \text{ tables/week}) (3 \text{ weeks}) = 150$ tables

New proposal

Cycle inventory $= \dfrac{Q}{2} = \dfrac{300}{2} = 150$ tables

Pipeline inventory $= dL = (50 \text{ tables/week}) (1 \text{ week}) = 50$ tables

The proposal would reduce total inventories and would have the added benefit of allowing 'House & Garden' to commit to orders much later.

Economic order quantity

The **Economic order quantity** (*EOQ*) is the order quantity that should minimise the total cost of inventory. The formula attempts to find the best balance between the advantages and disadvantages of holding stock. The key to finding *EOQ* is to determine the total cost of holding one unit in stock for a period of time (C_h) and the total costs of placing an order (C_o).

$$\text{Holding costs} = \text{holding cost/unit} \times \text{average inventory} = C_h \times \frac{Q}{2}$$

$$\text{Ordering costs} = \text{order cost} \times \text{number of orders placed} = C_o \times \frac{D}{Q}$$

$$\text{So, total cost, } C_t = \frac{C_h Q}{2} + \frac{C_o D}{Q}$$

To find out EOQ, we simply rearrange the formula:

$$Q_o = EOQ = \sqrt{\frac{2C_o D}{C_h}}$$

WORKED EXAMPLE

A local shop has a relatively stable demand for tins of sweetcorn throughout the year, with an annual total of 1,400 tins. The cost of placing an order is estimated at £15 and the annual cost of holding inventory is estimated at 25% of the product's value. The company purchases tins for 20p. We can work out how much the shop should order at a time as follows:

$$Q_o = EOQ = \sqrt{\frac{2C_o D}{C_h}}$$

$$Q_o = EOQ = \sqrt{\frac{2 \times 15 \times 1{,}400}{0.25 \times 0.2}} = \sqrt{\frac{42{,}000}{0.05}} = \sqrt{840{,}000} = 916.5$$

What is the total cost of this plan?

$$\text{Total cost, } C_t = \frac{C_h Q}{2} + \frac{C_o D}{Q} = \frac{0.05 \times 916.5}{2} + \frac{15 \times 1400}{916.5} = 22.66 + 22.91 = 45.57$$

Quantity discounts

Often suppliers will offer better prices if buyers are willing to buy in larger quantities. This creates a pressure towards holding higher levels of stock. Therefore, to find the best lot size one must compare the advantages of lower prices for purchases and fewer orders with the disadvantages of increased holding costs. Total annual costs now include not only holding costs and ordering costs, but also the cost of purchased items.

$$\text{So, total cost with quantity discounting } C_{tqd} = \frac{C_h Q}{2} + \frac{C_o D}{Q} + PD$$

Where P = per-unit price level.

The following 2-step procedure can be used to identify the best lot size where quantity discounting exists:

1 Begin with the *lowest price*, and calculate the EOQ for each price level until a feasible EOQ is found. It is feasible if it lies in the range corresponding to its price.

2 If the first feasible *EOQ* is for the *lowest price level*, this is the best lot size. If not, one must compare the total costs for the first feasible *EOQ* with the total costs for alternative price break quantities. The quantity with the lowest total cost is optimum.

WORKED EXAMPLE

A wine merchant has introduced quantity discounts to encourage larger order quantities for bottles of port. The discounts are shown below:

Order quantity	Price per bottle
0–100	€15.00
101–250	€13.50
250+	€11.00

Vital Wines estimates its annual demand at 1,500 bottles, its ordering costs are €30 per order, and its annual holding costs are 20% of the bottle's price.

Step 1 – find the feasible *EOQ*, starting with the lowest price:

$$EOQ_{€11.00} = \sqrt{\frac{2C_oD}{C_h}} = \sqrt{\frac{2\times 30\times 1,500}{0.2\times 11.0}} = \sqrt{\frac{90,000}{2.2}} = \sqrt{40,909.1} = 202.26$$

A 202-bottle order would actually cost €13.50 per bottle, instead of the €11.00 used to calculate *EOQ*, so this *EOQ* is not feasible. Now we try the next level.

$$EOQ_{€13.50} = \sqrt{\frac{2C_oD}{C_h}} = \sqrt{\frac{2\times 30\times 1,500}{0.2\times 13.50}} = \sqrt{\frac{90,000}{2.7}} = \sqrt{33,333.3} = 182.57$$

This quantity is feasible, because it lies in the range corresponding to its price.

Step 2 – compare the first feasible *EOQ* with the other price break quantities

Because the first feasible EOQ of €13.50 does not correspond with the lowest price level, we must compare its total cost with the price break quantity of 250+ at the lower price of €11.00.

$$C_t = \frac{C_hQ}{2} + \frac{C_oD}{Q} + PD$$

$$C_{€13.50} = \frac{C_hQ}{2} + \frac{C_oD}{Q} + PD = \frac{(0.2\times 13.50)(182.57)}{2} + \frac{(30\times 1,500)}{182.57} + (13.50\times 1,500) =$$

$$= 246.47 + 246.48 + 20,250 = 20,742.95$$

$$C_{€11.00} = \frac{C_hQ}{2} + \frac{C_oD}{Q} + PD = \frac{(0.2\times 11.00)(250.00)}{2} + \frac{(30\times 1,500)}{250.00} + (11.00\times 1,500)$$

$$= 275.00 + 180.00 + 16,500 = 16,955$$

Therefore, total costs, including the cost of purchases, will be minimised if Vital Wines buy in quantities of 250 to qualify for the best discount.

Economic batch quantity

When each complete replacement order arrives at one point in time, *EOQ* is an appropriate model to use in determining appropriate order volumes. However, in some cases, replenishment occurs over a time period rather than in one lot. The profiles of *EOQ* and *EBQ* are shown in Figures 4.1 and 4.2 below

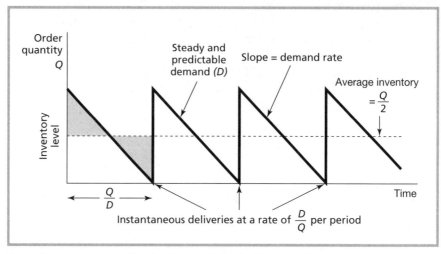

Figure 4.1 Inventory profiles chart the variation in inventory level

Source: Slack, N., Chambers, S. and Johnston, R. (2007) *Operations Management*, Fifth Edition. Harlow, UK: Pearson. Figure 12.5. p. 374. Reproduced with permission.

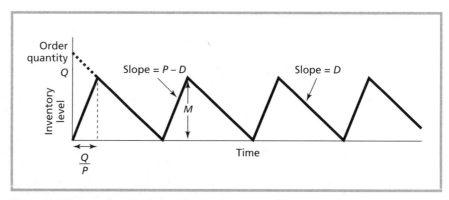

Figure 4.2 Inventory profile for gradual replacement of inventory

Source: Slack, N., Chambers, S. and Johnston, R. (2007) *Operations Management*, Fifth Edition. Harlow, UK: Pearson. Figure 12.8. p. 378. Reproduced with permission.

The gradual replacement profile is typical for cycle inventories supplied by batch processes, where items are produced internally and intermittently. The **economic batch quantity (*EBQ*)** is also sometimes known as the **economic manufacturing quantity (*EMQ*)**, **production order quantity (*POQ*)**, or the **economic production lot size (*ELS*)**. It is derived as follows:

$$EBQ = \sqrt{\frac{2C_o D}{C_h(1-(d/p))}}$$

Where d = demand per unit of time
p = production per unit of time
C_o = cost of ordering
C_h = cost of holding

WORKED EXAMPLE

A fruit canning plant in Johannesburg, South Africa has a single line for three different fruit types. Demand for each type of tin is reasonably constant at 50,000 per month (a month has 160 production hours). The tinning process rate is 1,200 per hour, but it takes 2 hours to clean and re-set between different runs. The cost of these changeovers (C_o) is calculated at £250 per hour. Stock-holding is calculated at $0.1 per tin per month.

First, we must ensure that d and p are in the same units (in this case per hour) *Note: the same goes for C_h and D (in this case calculated as per month). As long as these figures are in the same units, the equation works.*

$d = \dfrac{50,000}{160} = 312.5$ per hour

$p = 1,200$ per hour

$EBQ = \sqrt{\dfrac{2C_o D}{C_h(1-(d/p))}} = \sqrt{\dfrac{2 \times 250 \times 50,000}{0.1(1-(312.5/1,200))}} = \sqrt{\dfrac{25,000,000}{0.1(1-0.26)}} = \sqrt{\dfrac{25,000,000}{0.074}}$

$= \sqrt{337,837,837.8} = 18,380.37$ tins per batch

The timing decision

EOQ and *EBQ* help managers decide how much to order. The second important decision is when to place the order. In this section, we examine two types of inventory system – the **continuous review system (Q system)** and the **periodic review system (P system)**.

Continuous review (Q) system under certain conditions

A *Q* system, also called a **re-order point system**, determines the time of reorder based on the remaining level of inventory. A fixed quantity *Q* of an item is ordered when the inventory position reaches a predetermined minimum level. So, whilst the order quantity is fixed, the time between orders may differ. When demand is certain, the re-order point ($R_{certain}$) is calculated as follows:

$$R_{certain} = D \times L$$

Where D = average daily demand
L = lead time

> ### WORKED EXAMPLE
>
> A photography shop purchases memory cards in batches of 50. The average daily demand is for 6 memory cards and the lead time is 3 days:
>
> $R = D \times L = 6 \times 3 = 18$

Continuous review (Q) system under uncertain conditions

In reality, both lead time (t) and demand rate (d) often vary. This variability creates the need for safety stock, which can be set to give a predetermined likelihood of stock-outs occurring. So, when working in uncertain conditions, the re-order point ($R_{uncertain}$) is calculated as follows:

$$R_{uncertain} = (D \times L) + S$$

Where D = average daily demand
L = lead time
S = safety stock

The trade-off when deciding the level of safety stock is between customer service and inventory holding costs. A common approach used by operations managers is to set a service level – i.e. the desired probability of not running out of stock. This probability depends on variability, either in demand or in lead times. The greater the variation, the higher the safety stock required to ensure a set level of service. Assuming demand during lead time is normally distributed, we calculate safety stock (S) as follows:

$$S = z\sigma_L$$

Where z = number of standard deviations from the mean to implement the service level
σ_L = standard deviation in demand during lead-time

> ### WORKED EXAMPLE
>
> A packaging plant Abuja, Nigeria has daily demand for 5,000 type-A boxes, a 4-day lead time and a normally distributed demand pattern with standard deviation of 120. The company wants a service level of 99% (i.e. only a 1% probability that there will be a stock-out). Therefore, referring to the normal distribution table, the z value is 2.33 and safety stock is:
>
> $S = z\sigma_L = 2.33 \times 120 = 279.60$
>
> Therefore, the re-order point under this uncertainty is calculated as:
>
> $R_{uncertain} = (D \times L) + S = (5,000 \times 4) + 279.60 = 20,279.60$

Periodic (P) review system

An alternative to continuous review systems is a **periodic review system** or **P system**. Whilst a P system requires higher levels of safety stock than a Q system, it has the advantage of simplicity. In a P system, an order is always placed after each review and the time between reviews is fixed. Therefore, the order size (Q) may vary from one review to the next. When a predetermined time (P) has elapsed, an order is placed to ensure inventory is at the target level (T). The calculation below shows this:

$$Q = T - IP$$

Where T = target inventory position
IP = current inventory position ($=on$-$hand\ inventory + scheduled\ receipts - backorders$)

WORKED EXAMPLE

At the time of periodic review, an Italian convenience store has an in-hand inventory of 100 bags of crisps, no scheduled receipts, and a back-order for 15 bags. We can calculate how much should be ordered if the store has a target of 550 bags. The inventory position (IP) = 100 + 0 − 15 = 85. Therefore, the order quantity (Q) = $T - IP$ = 550 − 85 = 465 bags.

Questions

4.2.1 A kitchenware company located in Bonn, Germany has an average weekly demand for 70 toasters. Orders for these toasters have a lead time of 2 weeks and arrive in lots of 500. The company operates throughout the year, carries 4 days of inventory as safety stock and has no anticipation inventory. What is the average inventory held by the company?

4.2.2 What would be the effect if demand became less predictable, so safety stock increased to 10 days' demand, and if the lot size increased to 750?

4.2.3 Rive 1920 is an Italian firm making furniture which is shipped around the world. Its products' average cost is €4,000 and annual holding costs are calculated at 25%. Currently the firm uses overland transportation, which takes 5 days (pipeline inventory). Another option is to transport via airfreight. This will take 2 days, but will carry an additional cost of €50.00. Assuming the cost of ordering is the same, which option has the lower total costs?

4.2.4 Johnson & Johnson Inc. has relatively stable demand for its products throughout the year, with an annual total of 25,000 items. The cost of placing an order is estimated at €150 and the annual cost of holding inventory is estimated at 30% of any product's value. The company purchases the items for €240. How many items should the company order at a time? What is the total cost of this plan?

4.2.5 What would be the effect on holding costs, ordering costs and total costs if Johnson & Johnson had to order 500 items at a time?

4.2.6 Assuming annual demand for items increases from 25,000 to 35,000; the cost of holding stock is recalculated as 35% of the product value; and the cost of placing an order falls to €95, what is the new *EOQ*?

If the company have to order in batches of 50, how many items should they order at a time to minimise total costs?

4.2.7   Donningtons Ltd has a steady demand for 350 retro globes each year. Orders are calculated to cost $5 and the annual cost of holding stock is estimated at $15 per item. If the globe supplier has a minimum order size of 25 globes, how much more does it cost Donningtons Ltd relative to the optimum *EOQ*?

4.2.8   How many globes should the company order at a time if demand increases drastically to 1,600 and the cost of ordering falls from $5 to $4?

4.2.9   Greys Corp. assembles wind turbines. It has an annual demand of 6,700 for component 'Tynex' at a cost per item of €750. The cost of ordering is calculated as €50, whilst the estimated annual holding costs are 15% of the item cost. What is the *EOQ* for the 'Tynex' component?

4.2.10 The company has a choice between order sizes of 50 and 100. Which is the best choice?

4.2.11 Muesli Magic has an annual requirement for 800 tons of oats at a cost of $240 a ton. Orders costs $40 to place, whilst holding costs are calculated at $60 a ton. How many tons of oats should Muesli Magic order at a time?

4.2.12 If holding costs can be reduced to $40 a ton, what is the new *EOQ*?

4.2.13 What would be the *EOQ* if holding costs are $40 and demand increases to 2,800 tons per annum? What would be the total cost of inventory under these circumstances?

4.2.14 A toy distributor is offering quantity discounts for board games as follows:

Order quantity (games)	Price per game
0–50	$10.00
51–100	$9.00
100+	$8.00

Fleetwood Games, based in Chicago, USA, estimates its annual demand from this distributor at 680, its ordering costs are $10 and its annual holding costs at 25% of the game's price.

(a) Does the order quantity of 100+ give a feasible *EOQ*? If not, what price level does give a feasible *EOQ*?

(b) Which price level gives the lowest total cost?

4.2.15 A glass factory produces 4 different glass types on a single process line. It costs €1,000 every time production is switched, due to cleaning and re-setting. Monthly stock holding costs are estimated at €0.3 per item and monthly demand is estimated at 400,000 per item. The factory works an average of 28 days per month and 20 hours per day. The process rate per hour of production is 5,000 items. Determine the economic batch size.

$$d = \frac{400,000}{28 \times 20} = 714 \text{ per hour}$$

$p = 5,000$ per hour

4.2.16 What is the effect on the EBQ is the cost of switching production falls from €1,000 to €500 and monthly demand falls from 400,000 per item to 375,000?

4.2.17 What is the EBQ if switching costs fall further to €300; the cost of holding stock falls from €0.3 to €0.25; demand remains constant at 375,000 items per month; and production per hour increases to 5,500?

4.2.18 Top Hatz Inc. makes a variety of ski hats. The average demand for the 'Nordic Dream' hat is 125 per week and production is capable of producing 500 hats per week. Set-up cost is €245. The value of the finished hats is €25 and the annual holding cost per item is 20% of its value.

(a) What is the economic batch quantity?
(b) What is the production time for each cycle?
(c) What is the average time between orders (*TBO*), assuming there are 350 days available per year?

4.2.19 Top Hatz Inc.'s average demand for the 'Nordic Dream' hat increases to 350 per week; its production capability improves to 700 hats per week; set-up cost falls to €95;, and the annual holding cost per item increases to 35% of its value. What is the effect on *EBQ*, production time for each cycle and average time between orders?

4.2.20 A car manufacturer purchases windscreen wipers in batches of 3,000. The average daily demand is 500 and the lead time is 4 days. Assuming the use of continuous review with no safety stock, what is the re-order point?

4.2.21 What is the effect on the re-order point if average daily demand increases to 575, but the lead time drops to 3 days?

4.2.22 A sandwich company has an average hourly demand for 223 prawn sandwiches, a 2-hour lead time and a normally distributed demand pattern with standard deviation of 45. The company wants a service level of 95% (*z* value = 1.65). What is the re-order point in this situation?

4.2.23 A chocolate shop has an average daily demand for 67 bars of white chocolate, a 4-day lead time, and a normally distributed demand pattern with standard deviation of 23. The shop wants a 90% service level (*z* value = 1.28). There are currently 305 bars in the store. Should the manager place a new order?

4.2.24 What would the re-order point be if the chocolate shop's average demand during lead time increased to 75; its standard deviation increased to 30; the service level requirement increased to 95% (*z* = 1.65); but the lead time was cut to 2 days?

4.2.25 A small shop has a weekly demand for 15 teapots and a lead time of 2.5 weeks. What is the re-order point for these items?

4.2.26 It turns out that the shop has normally distributed demand with a standard deviation during the lead time of 4 teapots. The company wish to ensure that stock-outs only occur 10% of the time during lead time (*z* value = 1.28). What is the new re-order point?

4.2.27 At the time of periodic review, a book shop had an in-hand inventory of 3 maps of New York, a scheduled receipt of 5 maps and no back-orders. Given a target of 12 maps how many maps should be ordered?

4.3 Linear programming

Operations management is concerned with the transformation of input resources into output products and services. Operations managers ensure that these resources are used as effectively as possible, producing a mixture of products and/or services that best contributes to the operations' overall objectives. **Linear programming (LP)** is a mathematical technique that aims to help operations managers by optimising how resources are used within an operation.

Maximising problems

Linear programming is best understood by following a simple example. Whilst it is much simpler than the sort of things linear programming is used for in practice, its relative simplicity allows us to demonstrate how the method works through a simple graphical formulation.

WORKED EXAMPLE

A company produces podcasts and videos for the education market. Both podcasts and videos need studio time to record the basic material followed by editing time that cuts the recorded material and produces a finished product.

Podcasts take 3 hours of studio time and 6 hours of editing time each. Videos take 5 hours of studio time but only 3 hours of editing time each. For every video product produced, the company receives €1,600 and for every podcast the company receives €1,200.

The company has to book time in the studio and in the editing suite in advance. Next month it has booked 57 hours of studio time and 72 hours of time in the editing suite. Business is good and customers are prepared to wait for the finished products. We can calculate how many podcasts and how many videos the company should produce in the next month in order to maximise its revenue.

Establishing the constraints to a feasible solution

The first step in any linear programme problem is to establish the constraints on the feasible set of solutions. By this we mean finding out what the company could do and what they can't do because of some kind of resource limitation. In this case we are told of two constraints:

- The studio time that can be used by the company in the next month must be ≤ 57 hours (the amount of time they have booked in the studio).
- The amount of time spent on editing the products must be ≤ 72 hours (the amount of time they have booked in the editing suite)

If, $p =$ the number of podcasts produced in the month, and

$v =$ the number of videos produced in the month,

given that podcasts take 3 hours of studio time and videos take 5 hours of studio time, and we have 57 hours in total available in the month, the constraint on studio time can be expressed as:

$3p + 5v \leq 57$

Similarly, given that the podcasts require 6 hours of editing time and videos require 3 hours of editing time each, and given that we have 72 hours of editing suite time available, then the constraint on editing suite time can be expressed as follows:

$6p + 3v \leq 72$

Worked example *continued*

It is easier to understand linear programming if we express these algebraic functions graphically. Figure 4.3 shows the constraint on studio time graphically. This graph can be simply constructed by first assuming that we don't produce any podcasts, in other words, $p = 0$.
When $p = 0$:

$(3 \times 0) + 5v = 57$

Therefore, $v = 57/5 = 11.4$

This gives the point at which the line intersects the v axis.
Similarly, when $v = 0$:

$3p + (5 \times 0) = 57$

Therefore, $p = 57/3 = 19$

This gives the point at which the line crosses the p axis.
So, in order to keep within the constraints on studio time, whatever number of podcasts and videos is produced must lie within the shaded area in Figure 4.3. Any combination of p and v outside this area would exceed the maximum amount of time available in the studio.

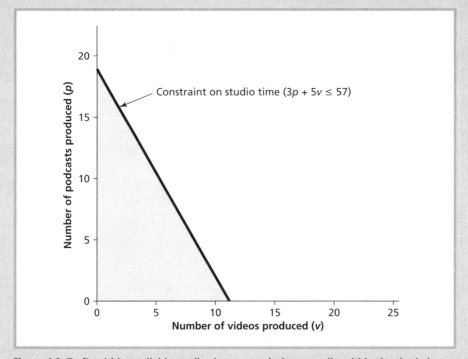

Figure 4.3 To fit within available studio time, any solution must lie within the shaded area

We can also plot graphically the constraints on editing time. Figure 4.4 shows the constraint on studio time graphically. Given that podcasts require 6 hours of editing time and videos require 3 hours of video time and the maximum amount of time in the editing suite is 72 hours,

$6p + 3v \leq 72$

Worked example *continued*

Again, the graph of this function can be simply constructed by first assuming that we don't produce any podcasts, in other words, $p = 0$.

When $p = 0$:

$$(6 \times 0) + 3v = 72$$

Therefore, $v = 72/3 = 24$

This gives the point at which the line intersects the v axis.

Similarly, when $v = 0$:

$$6p + (3 \times 0) = 72$$

Therefore, $p = 72/6 = 12$

This gives the point at which the line crosses the p axis.

So, in order to keep within the constraints on editing time, whatever number of podcasts and videos is produced must lie within the shaded area in Figure 4.4. Any combination of p and v outside this area would exceed the maximum amount of time available in the studio.

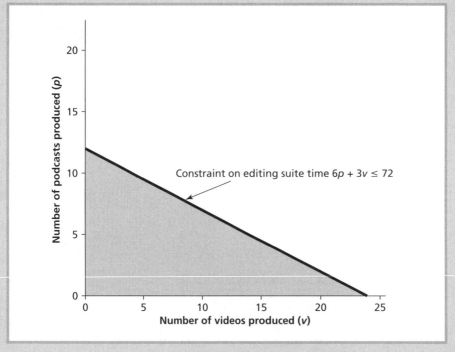

Figure 4.4 To fit within available editing time, any solution must lie within the shaded area

But, to be feasible the combination of podcasts and videos must lie within *both* the constraints on the studio time and the constraints on the editing suite. This is shown in Figure 4.5 as the double shaded area defined by the points A, B, C and D.

Worked example *continued*

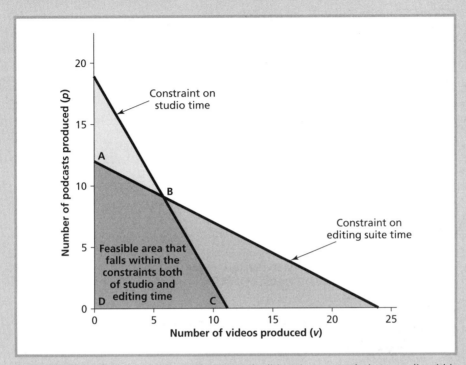

Figure 4.5 To fit within available studio time and editing time, any solution must lie within the double shaded area

Adding the objective function

Now that we have found the area representing the feasible solutions, we can start to find the optimal (best) solution. To do this we need to establish what is known as the **objective function**. This is the mathematical equation that states the objective (usually some financial measure such as profit) in terms of the resources that we are allocating (in this case the values of p and v). It is this mathematical equation that we are trying to optimise. In this case the objective is to maximise revenue.

One method of finding the point within the area of feasible solutions that optimises our objective is to draw a line that represents all the possible combinations of p and v that result in a given benefit (in this case a given revenue). This is called the **iso-benefit line**. It could be, for example, an **iso-cost line** that we are trying to minimise, or an **iso-profit line** that we are trying to maximise. Here it is an **iso-revenue line** that we are trying to maximise.

So, revenue, $R = €1{,}200p + €1{,}600v$

For example, a single line that represents all the combinations of p and v that give a revenue of €19,200 will be expressed as:

$$19{,}200 = 1{,}200p + 1{,}600v$$

To draw this, first set $p = 0$ to find where the line intersects the v axis.

$$19{,}200 = (1{,}200 \times 0) + 1{,}600v$$

Therefore, $v = 19{,}200/1{,}600$

$$v = 12$$

Worked example *continued*

Next, set $v = 0$ to find where the line intersects the p axis.

$19,200 = 1,200p + (1,600 \times 0)$

Therefore, $p = 19,200/1,200$

$p = 16$

If we were to go through the same procedure to draw an iso-revenue line for $R = €25,000$ it would connect the points $p = 0$, $v = 15.625$, and $p = 20.833$, $v = 0$. Both these iso-revenue lines are shown in Figure 4.6.

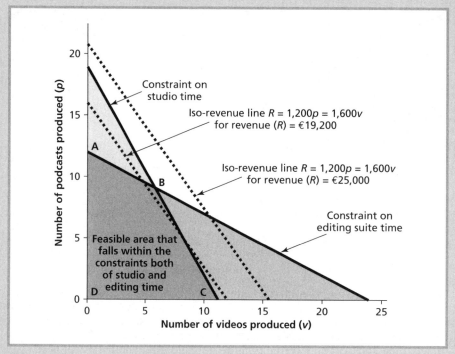

Figure 4.6 Iso-revenue lines indicate the optimum point within the feasible area (in this case, point B)

Note that these lines are parallel, as they always will be when it is only the value of R that is changing. The real benefit of drawing these iso-benefit lines is that they indicate where the optimum solution will be. In this case, the optimum solution will lie at point B because moving the iso-revenue line any further to the right (by increasing the value of R) than the point when it passes through B will move it beyond the area of feasible solutions (area ABCD). Conversely, moving the line to the left (by reducing the value of R) will only create the potential for revenue to be increased by moving the line back to the right.

The next step is to find the exact coordinates of point B. This will occur when *both* constraint expressions, as equations, are satisfied. That is, we need to solve the simultaneous equations:

$3p + 5v = 57$ equation 4a

$6p + 3v = 72$ equation 4b

Worked example *continued*

From equation 4a,

$3p = 57 - 5v$

$p = (57 - 5v)/3$

Substituting into equation 4b,

$$\frac{6(57 - 5v)}{3} + 3v = 72$$

$114 - 10v + 3v = 72$

$7v = 42$

$v = 6$

Substituting back into equation 4a

$3p + 5 \times 6 = 57$

$$p = \frac{57 - 30}{3}$$

$$p = 9$$

So, the optimal combination of podcasts and videos that will maximise revenues is 9 podcasts and 6 videos.

Adding more constraints

Constraints are not always a function of all the decision variables (in this case p and v). They may be a function of only one variable.

For example, suppose the company's operations schedulers now find out that their sales staff have made a firm promise to customers that will definitely deliver a minimum of 9 videos within the planning period. Now we have a new constraint of:

v is ≥ 9

This new constraint is shown in Figure 4.7. Unfortunately, adding this new constraint reduces further the area of feasible solutions. Now the only solutions that meet all the constraints are within the area EFC. More importantly, the previously optimum solution of $p = 9$, $v = 6$ is now outside the feasible area. Observing the slope of the iso-revenue line, it is now point E that represents the optimum solution. At point E, $v = 9$ (because it is on the new constraint line of $v \geq 9$).

Point E is also on the studio constraint line of:

$3p + 5v = 57$

Therefore, when $v = 9$

$$p = \frac{57 - (5 \times 9)}{3}$$

$$p = 4$$

Therefore, the new optimal solution is when $v = 9$ and $p = 4$.

Worked example *continued*

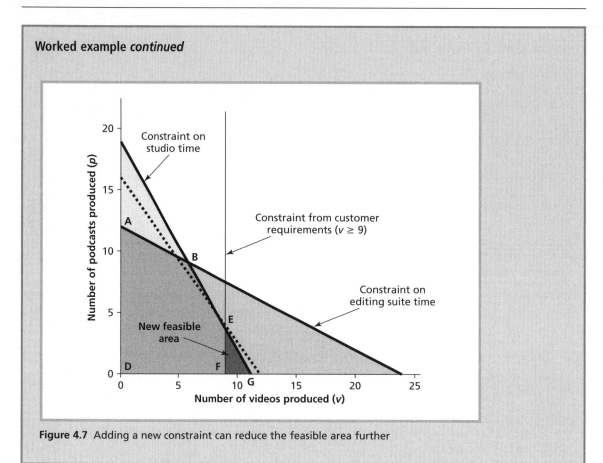

Figure 4.7 Adding a new constraint can reduce the feasible area further

Minimising problems

The previous example illustrated how a simple graphical representation of linear programming is used when the objective is to maximise some function such as revenue or profit. However, sometimes we need to minimise an objective such as the number of people employed or total cost. The principle when minimisation is involved is essentially the same as when we are trying to maximise an objective function. However, this time areas of feasibility defined by the constraints are usually to the right of the equation that defines them and we are trying to find an optimum point to the left or below the area of feasibility that minimises the objective function.

WORKED EXAMPLE

Suppose a llama-breeding operation is trying to minimise the cost of feeding its animals whilst ensuring that they receive at least the minimum of dietary nutrition. To keep things simple let us assume that there are only two available makes of llama feed, Llam-a-grub and Dellama. It is important that the animals receive three dietary ingredients, which we shall call A, B and C. The table below indicates the quantity of each ingredient (in grams/kilo) contained in each make of llama feed. It also shows the minimum quantity

Worked example *continued*

of each ingredient that each animal must receive every day. The cost of Llam-a-grub is €0.2/kilo and the cost of Dellama is €0.4/kilo.

Dietary ingredients in the two available makes of llama feed

Available llama feeds	Ingredient A grams/kilo	Ingredient B grams/kilo	Ingredient C grams/kilo
Llam-a-grub	5	4	1
Dellama	10	3	0
Minimum quantity of each ingredient per animal	80	36	2

Figure 4.8 illustrates this problem graphically. There are three constraints that indicate the minimum amount of each ingredient that each animal must receive every day.

If L = the amount of Llam-a-grub to be fed to each llama every day in kilos, and
D = the amount of Dellama to be fed to each llama every day in kilos, then, for each animal to receive a minimum of 80g of ingredient A, then,

$5L + 10D \geq 80$

For each animal to receive a minimum of 36g of ingredient B, then,

$4L + 3D \geq 36$

For each animal to receive a minimum of 2g of ingredient C, then,

$L \geq 2$

The shaded area in Figure 4.8 is the area that contains all feasible solutions.

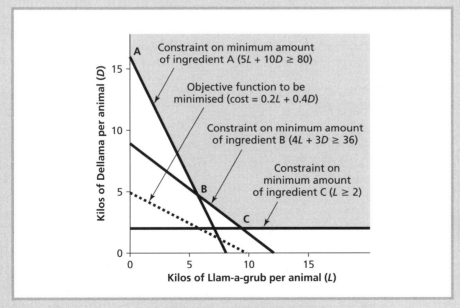

Figure 4.8 Graphical representation of the Llama feed problem

Worked example *continued*

We must find the point at which cost is minimised where:

Cost = 0.2L + 0.4D

The dotted line in Figure 4.8 shows this cost function when the cost is €2. And although the minimum feasible cost point is not on this line, it does show that the optimum will be at point C. Point C is where the constraint line for Ingredient B and constraint line for Ingredient C intersect. To find this point we must solve the simultaneous equations,

4L + 3D = 36
D = 2

Solving these equations gives point C as D = 2 (not surprisingly) and L = 9.333. Therefore, the minimum cost solution that will provide the animals with adequate quantities of ingredients A, B and C and yet minimise cost is by feeding them 2 kilos of Dellama and 9.333 kilos of Llam-a-grub each day.

The general form of linear programming problems

We have limited the two problems described so far to those involving two variables. In practice, real **linear programming problems** often involve many variables as well as many constraints. And although it is not possible to draw graphical solutions, it is possible to imagine them in n-dimensional space. Yet it is still possible to solve multi-variable problems using a procedure called the **Simplex method**. Essentially the Simplex method does exactly what we have done graphically. It examines each corner of the feasible area (in n-dimensional space) until it finds the best solution, that is the one that maximises or minimises the objective function. There are several computer programs that solve multi-dimensional problems. For example, Excel spreadsheets have a built-in problem-solving procedure called Solver. Essentially these programs solve the following generic problem.

Optimise an objective function Z, where

$$Z = aX_1 + bX_2 + cX_3 + \ldots\ldots\ldots\ldots nX_N$$

Subject to the constraints,

$$lX_1 + mX_2 + nX_3 + \ldots\ldots\ldots\ldots tX_N \leq \text{ or } \geq C_1$$
$$pX_1 + qX_2 + rX_3 + \ldots\ldots\ldots\ldots zX_N \leq \text{ or } \geq C_2$$

etc.

Questions

4.3.1 Minimise cost, where the objective function for cost $(C) = x + 4y$.

$x + y \leq 10$
$5x + 2y \geq 20$
$2y - x \geq 0$
$x \geq 0, y \geq 0$

4.3.2 Maximise the objective function, $Z = 3x + 5y$, subject to the following constraints:

$x + y \leq 5$
$2x + y \geq 4$
$x \geq 0, y \geq 0$

4.3.3 Minimise the objective function, $4a + 5b + 6c$, subject to the constraints:

$a + b \geq = 11$
$a - b \leq = 5$
$c - a - b = 0$
$7a \geq = 35 - 12b$
$a \geq = 0 \; b \geq = 0 \; c \geq = 0$

4.3.4 Maximise the objective function $5X_1 + 6X_2$ subject to the constraints

$X_1 + X_2 \leq = 10$
$X_1 - X_2 \geq = 3$
$5X_1 + 4X_2 \leq = 35$
$X_1 \geq = 0$
$X_2 \geq = 0$

4.3.5 A company makes two products (P and Q) using two machines (X and Y). Each unit of P that is produced requires 50 minutes of processing time on machine X and 30 minutes of processing time on machine Y. Each unit of Q that is produced requires 24 minutes of processing time on machine X and 33 minutes of processing time on machine Y.

At the start of the current week there are 30 units of P and 90 units of Q in stock. Available processing time on machine X is forecast to be 40 hours and on machine Y is forecast to be 35 hours.

The demand for P in the current week is forecast to be 75 units and for Q is forecast to be 95 units. Company policy is to maximise the combined sum of the units of P and the units of Q in stock at the end of the week. What are the values for P and Q and the value of the objective function?

4.3.6 A laboratory breeds baby crocodiles to test toothpaste on. Accurate test results depend on the crocodiles being in the best possible health. To achieve this crocodiles must have a daily diet containing a minimum of 24 grams (g) of fat, 36 g of carbohydrates, and 4 g of protein. But the crocodiles should be fed no more than five blocks of food a day.

Two types of crocodile food are available on the market sold in standard 'blocks', Food A and Food B. Food A contains 8 g of fat, 12 g of carbohydrates, and 2 g of protein per block, and costs $0.20 per block. Food B contains 12 g of fat, 12 g of carbohydrates, and 1 g of protein per block, at a cost of $0.30 per block.

How much of each food should the crocs be fed?

4.3.7 At a chemical plant, the process requires the production of at least two litres of chemical A for each litre of chemical B. To meet the anticipated demand, at least 3,000 litres a day will need to be produced. The demand for chemical A, on the other hand, is not more than 6.4 thousand litres a day.

If chemical A is selling for €1.90 per litre and chemical B sells for €1.50 per litre, how much of each should be produced in order to maximise revenue?

4.3.8 Marie needs to buy some storage boxes. Marie knows that Box X costs €10 per unit, requires 6 square metres of floor space and holds 8 cubic metres of files. Box Y costs €20 per unit, requires 8 square metres of floor space and holds 12 cubic metres of files. Marie has a budget of €140 for this purchase, though she does not have to spend the entire budget. The office has room for no more than 72 square metres of box space. How many of which type of box should Marie buy, in order to maximise storage volume?

4.3.9 A tourist shop in Paris sells models of Notre Dame and models of the Eiffel Tower. It costs €20 to purchase each model of Notre Dame and it takes 2 hours to paint it. It costs €25 to purchase each model of the Eiffel Tower and it takes 5 hours to paint it. The shop has at most €400 to spend and at most 60 hours to frame paintings. It makes €30 profit on each model of Notre Dame and €50 profit on each model of the Eiffel Tower. How many models of each tourist attraction should the shop purchase if it wishes to maximise profits?

4.3.10 The Stockholm machine company produces two items (X and Y). The resources needed to produce X and Y are 'machine time' and 'craft time' for hand finishing. Each item of X requires 13 minutes of machine time and 20 minutes of craft time. Each item of Y requires 19 minutes of machine time and 29 minutes of craft time.

The company has 40 hours of machine time available in the next working week but only 35 hours of craftsman time. Machine time is costed at SEK10 per hour worked and craftsman time is costed at SEK2 per hour worked. Both machine and craftsman idle times incur no costs. The revenue received for each item produced (all production is sold) is SEK20 for X and SEK30 for Y. The company has a specific contract to produce 10 items of X per week for a particular customer.

How many of X and Y should the company produce per week?

4.3.11 A company manufactures two products (A and B) and the profit per unit sold is €3 and €5 respectively. Each product has to be assembled on a particular machine, each unit of product A taking 12 minutes of assembly time and each unit of product B 25 minutes of assembly time. The company estimates that the machine used for assembly has an effective working week of only 30 hours (due to maintenance/breakdown).

Technological constraints mean that for every five units of product A produced at least two units of product B must be produced.

1 How much of each product should be produced?
2 The company has been offered the chance to hire an extra machine, thereby doubling the effective assembly time available. What is the *maximum* amount you would be prepared to pay (per week) for the hire of this machine and why?

4.4 Transportation method

One particular type of linear programming problem can be solved using a simplified version of the simplex approach. This is called the **transportation method** because it is used to solve problems involving several sources of products or services and several destinations of products or services. Although it can be used to represent more general problems, its most common application is to problems involving transporting products from several sources to several destinations. The usual objective of transportation problems is to minimise the cost of shipping X units to Y destinations.

There are four steps in solving transportation problems.

Step 1 – Collect data regarding the ability of each source to supply; the requirements of each destination; and the costs involved in supplying each destination from each source (this is sometimes called the 'transportation tableau').

Step 2 – Establish an initial feasible solution that satisfies the ability of each source to supply the requirements of each destination.

Step 3 – Develop a better solution.

Step 4 – Move incrementally to the optimal solution.

We will discuss each step by using a simple example, shown in Figure 4.9. A company has three manufacturing plants located at Rouen, Metz and Essen. We will assume that all products made at the three plants are broadly similar and measured in 'units'. Rouen has 35 units of capacity, Metz 20 units of capacity and Essen 50 units of capacity per period. All three plants supply three warehouses located at Gent, Aachen and Frankfurt. The warehouse at Gent requires 45 units per period; the warehouse at Aachen requires 30 units per period; and the one at Frankfurt also requires 30 units per period. The cost of transporting between the plants and the warehouses depends on which plant is supplying which warehouse. The overall objective is to allocate the capacity at each plant to supplying one or more of the warehouses so that the total cost of transportation is minimised.

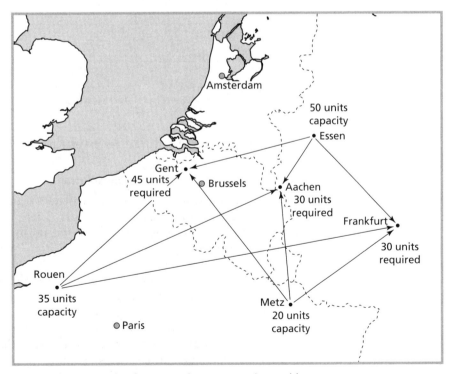

Figure 4.9 An example of an example transportation problem

Step 1 – Collect data for the 'transportation tableau'

The transportation tableau shows the data regarding the ability of each source to supply, the requirements of each destination, and the costs involved in supplying each destination from each source. Conventionally, supply availability at each source is shown in the far right column and the destination requirement is shown in the bottom row; each cell then represents a unique route. The unit transportation cost is shown in the upper right corner of the cell and the quantity of 'flow' on each route is shown in the centre of the cell. For our example problem, the transportation tableau is shown in Figure 4.10.

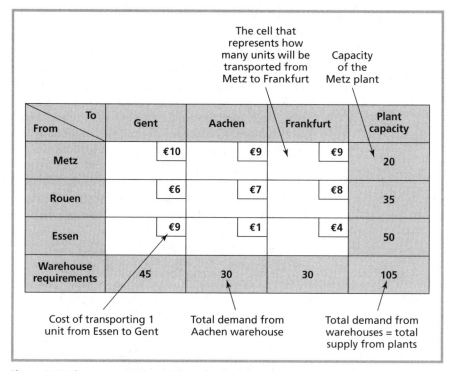

Figure 4.10 The transportation tableau for the example transportation problem

Step 2 – Establish an initial feasible solution

Developing an initial feasible solution involves assigning numbers to cells to satisfy both supply and demand constraints. There are several methods for doing this. Amongst the most common are the **northwest-corner method** and the **least-cost method**.

The northwest-corner method is probably the most straightforward way of allocating (in this case) products to routes. It simply involves starting at the top left-hand cell (the northwest corner of the matrix). See Figure 4.11. In our example this cell represents the route between Metz and Gent. Product is allocated to this cell such that all requirements are satisfied for the destination, or (as in this case) all capacity is used from the source. This means allocating 20 units into this cell. This exhausts the capacity from Metz, but still leaves Gent short of 25 units. These can be allocated from the capacity at Rouen as shown. The requirements of Gent are now fully satisfied and

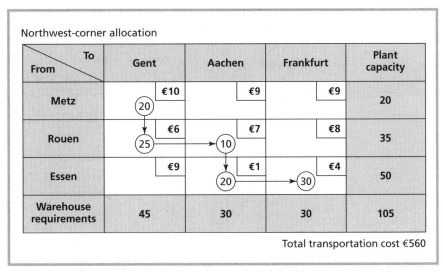

Figure 4.11 The initial feasible solution for the example transportation problem using the 'northwest-corner' method

Rouen has 10 units of capacity left to allocate. These can be allocated to supplying Aachen, which exhausts the capacity of Rouen but leaves Aachen with 20 units required. These are allocated from Essen, whose remaining 30 units are allocated to Frankfurt. This completes the allocation with all sources used and all destinations' requirements satisfied. It results in a total transportation cost of €516.

The obvious flaw with this method of achieving an initial allocation is that its sole objective is to lie within the constraints imposed by capacity and requirements. It makes absolutely no attempt to minimise costs. An alternative method of achieving an initial allocation of products to routes is called the least-cost method. Very simply, this first of all identifies the lowest-cost route, allocates as much to that as is possible, then moves on to the next lowest-cost route, and so on until everything has been allocated. In this case (see Figure 4.12) the lowest-cost route is between Essen and Aachen which costs only €1 per unit. The maximum that can be allocated to that cell is 30 units which satisfy Aachen's requirements. The next lowest-cost route is that between Essen and Frankfurt which costs €4 per unit. Essen only has 20 units of capacity remaining which does not satisfy Frankfurt's requirements totally but nevertheless can be allocated in order, partially, to satisfy Frankfurt's requirements. The third lowest-cost route is that between Rouen and Gent and 35 units can be allocated to this cell. This procedure continues until all requirements are satisfied. In this case, the total transportation cost using the least-cost method has reduced to €516. However, the least-cost method does not guarantee to provide the optimal (best) solution. Therefore, we need to test to see whether adjusting our initial solution can provide a better one.

Step 3 – Develop a better solution

The final step in the transportation method is to check to see if the current allocation of products to routes can be improved upon. If it can, then this improvement is made and, again, a check is made to see if further improve-

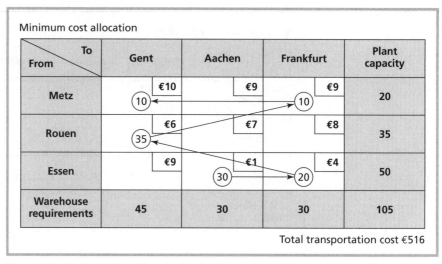

Figure 4.12 The initial feasible solution for the example transportation problem using the 'least-cost' method

ment can be achieved. This continues until no further improvements can be achieved. The method used to do this is known as the **'stepping stone' method**. It is a relatively straightforward, intuitively obvious, but rather laborious method. The stepping stone method operates as follows.

(a) Choose any of the currently unused cells in the tableau to evaluate.

(b) Starting at this cell, find a closed path that leads back to the original cell, using only squares that are currently being used, and using only horizontal and vertical moves. (It is, however, permissible to step over cells, either empty ones or occupied ones.)

(c) Put a + sign in the unused cell (indicating a very small addition of products to this cell). Put a – sign in the next cell on the path (indicating a very small reduction in products allocated to this route) and so on until you return to the original empty cell.

(d) Calculate the 'improvement index' of making this small change by adding the unit cost figures in all the cells with a + sign and subtracting from them the sum of the unit cost figures in each cell containing a – sign. If this improvement index is 0 or positive it means that making any small change will increase the total cost of transportation. If the improvement index is negative it means that making a change will reduce the total costs. Therefore, any negative improvement indices indicate that the current allocation is not optimal and can be improved.

(e) Repeat this procedure for all the other empty cells and calculate the improvement index for each. If there are no negative improvement indices the current allocation is optimal. If there is at least one negative improvement index then the current allocation can be improved. Choose the cell with the most negative improvement index and make the maximum change possible within the constraints. Then repeat the procedure (a) to (e) until no further improvement can be made.

Figure 4.13 illustrates how the stepping stone method can be used to investigate one currently empty cell in our previous allocation. This cell is that representing the route between Metz and Aachen. A + sign is put into this cell, a – sign is put into the route between Metz and Frankfurt, a + sign into the route between Essen and Frankfurt, and a – sign into the route between Essen and Aachen. Thus, we have traced a route using only occupied cells and vertical or horizontal moves back to the empty cell. We can now calculate the improvement index as follows.

$$\text{Improvement index} = (9 + 4) - (9 + 1) = 3$$

In fact, in this case, none of the currently empty cells provides a negative improvement index. Therefore, the current allocation cannot be improved upon and must be optimal.

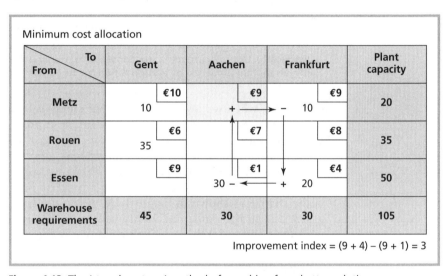

Figure 4.13 The 'stepping stone' method of searching for a better solution

Step 4 – Move incrementally to the optimal solution

In order to illustrate how an improvement can be made, observe the tableau in Figure 4.14. It has three sources, A, B and C, and three destinations, X, Y and Z. In the initial allocation cell CX is empty. We can put a + sign in this cell and trace a path back to the cell through CY, AY, and AX. This provides an improvement index as follows.

$$\text{Improvement index} = (8 + 5) - (10 + 4) = -1$$

Therefore, allocating products into cell CX, which is currently empty, will reduce the total cost. Now look at the positives and negatives in the cell used to trace the path to and from CX, move the allocation of 15 units from AX to CX, reduce the allocation of 15 in CY and move it to join the currently allocated 5 units in AY. This results in a total allocation in cell AY of 20 units. This represents the maximum change we can make using only the cells with + or – signs in them. And, as can be seen, it does reduce the total cost.

Initial total costs = $15 \times 4 + 5 \times 5 + 35 \times 3 + 15 \times 10 + 30 \times 11 = 670$

New total cost = $35 \times 3 + 15 \times 8 + 20 \times 5 + 30 \times 11 = 655$

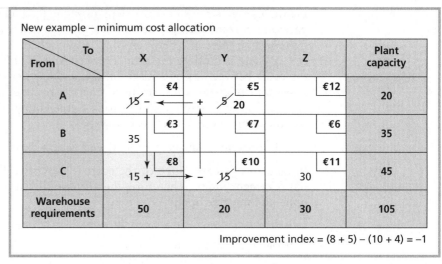

Figure 4.14 Using the stepping stone method to examine the initially empty square CX, reveals that the total cost of transportation can be further reduced.

In fact, when we investigate the other empty cells we find that moving any units to them does not result in a negative improvement index. Therefore, with this initial allocation the move we have just made is the only improvement we can make at this stage. Nevertheless, once we have made that change we must look to see if, having made the change, any further improvement can be made. This actually leaves us with a problem because, now we have made the change as shown in Figure 4.14, we do not have sufficient cells filled to test out all the remaining empty cells using the rules of the stepping stone method outlined previously. This condition is known as **degeneracy**.

Degeneracy

The stepping stone method of searching for incremental improvement relies on the ability to trace a path back to each empty cell using only vertical and horizontal moves and using only occupied cells as 'turning points' on the path. This in turn depends on the number of occupied cells being equal to the number of rows in the tableau plus the number of columns in the tableau minus one. A solution that does not satisfy this rule is called degenerate.

In fact degeneracy is relatively easily coped with. We simply artificially create an occupied cell by placing a very small amount (almost 0) that we can in effect call 0 that represents a 'fake' shipment. We can then treat this cell as if it had a real allocation. Figure 4.15 illustrates this. So, to investigate the currently empty cell AZ using the stepping stone method there is no way that one can trace a path back to the cell using only currently occupied cells. However, if we place a very small amount of production into cell CY (call it almost 0) we can use the stepping stone method as previously explained. In this case, investigating this cell provides an improvement index of 8. Therefore, no improvement would be made by allocating any production to it. (However, you may like to try to use the stepping stone method on the other cells to see whether further improvements can be made.)

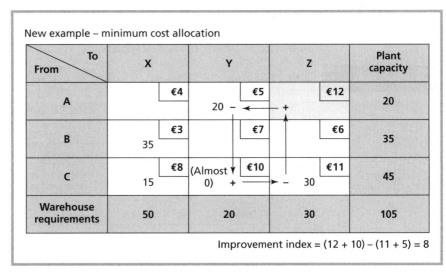

Figure 4.15 Coping with degeneracy by allocating a very small amount (almost 0) of production to an empty cell

Supply and demand not equal

So far we have assumed that whatever is required by destinations exactly matches whatever can be supplied by sources. Yet this is not always so. Sometimes demand and supply are not equal. This is not difficult to handle within the transportation method. It is done simply by introducing dummy sources or dummy destinations to absorb surplus demand or supply. The cells within these dummy rows or columns are given a cost equal to 0 (because in reality there will be no production using these dummy routes). Figure 4.16 illustrates how this can work. In this case there is a surplus of supply over demand. The sum total of plant capacity from plants A, B and C equals 155 units, whereas the total requirements from destinations X, Y and

New example – minimum cost allocation

To\From	X	Y	Z	Dummy	Plant capacity
A	€6	€5 — 60	€10	0	60
B	€4 — 40	€7	€8 — 10	0	50
C	€11	€10	€9 — 30	0 — 15	45
Warehouse requirements	40	60	40	15	155

Figure 4.16 Using dummies to allow for uneven supply and demand

Z is only 140 units. We have therefore allocated a dummy destination to absorb the surplus 15 units of supply. In this particular case, source C is not fully used to supply the real destinations.

Questions

4.4.1 (a) Using the northwest-corner approach to the transportation problem below, what is the total cost?

(b) Using the least-cost approach to the transportation problem below, what is the total cost?

	X	Y	Z	Supply
A	4	8	6	40
B	6	3	7	30
C	9	5	2	20
Demand	40	35	15	

4.4.2 (a) Using the northwest-corner approach to the transportation problem below, what is the total cost?

(b) Using the least-cost approach to the transportation problem below, what is the total cost?

	X	Y	Z	Supply
A	1	9	6	120
B	6	3	8	50
C	2	5	4	70
Demand	100	90	50	

4.4.3 Give an initial solution to the transportation tableau shown below, using the lowest-cost approach.

	X	Y	Z	Supply
A	2	8	1	10
B	6	3	2	30
C	4	5	6	20
Demand	20	20	20	60

4.4.4 Find the optimum solution to the following transportation problem (note, a dummy row will be needed).

	P	Q	R	S	Supply
A	10	30	25	15	14
B	20	15	20	10	10
C	10	30	20	20	15
D	30	40	35	45	12
Demand	10	15	12	15	

4.4.5 Four factories, in London (capacity 15), Slough (capacity 6), Hull (capacity 14) and York (capacity 11), supply four distribution centres in Canterbury (requirements 10), Wells (requirements 12), Cardiff (requirements 15) and Peebles (requirements 9). The costs of transporting from each factory to each distribution centre (in the order listed above) are as follows: London 25, 35, 36, 60; Slough 55, 30, 25, 25; Hull 40, 50, 80, 90; York 30, 40, 66, 75. What is the cost for the optimum solution?

CHAPTER 5

Answers

1.1   Time series analysis

1.1.1 $(46 + 54 + 46)/3 = 48.67$

1.1.2 $(38 + 46 + 54)/3 = 46$

1.1.3 $(0.6 \times 38) + (0.2 \times 46) + (0.2 \times 54) = 42.8$

1.1.4 $\dfrac{113 + 110 + 124}{3} = 115.67$

1.1.5 $\dfrac{132 + 113 + 110 + 124 + 145}{5} = 124.8$

1.1.6

Year	Demand	3-year moving ave
1	58	
2	76	
3	87	
4	91	73.67
5	98	84.67
6	113	92
7	167	100.67
8		126

1.1.7

Year	Demand	3-year weighted moving ave
1	58	
2	76	
3	87	
4	91	80.8
5	98	88.8
6	113	94.8
7	167	106.3
8		143.9

1.1.8 Year 9 forecast = $(0.6 \times 145) + (0.3 \times 167) + (0.1 \times 113) = 148.4$

1.1.9 146.2

1.1.10 $F_t = \alpha(A_{t-1}) + (1 - \alpha)F_{t-1} = (0.3 \times 267) + (0.7 \times 250) = 255.1$

1.1.11 $F_t = \alpha(A_{t-1}) + (1 - \alpha)F_{t-1} = (0.4 \times 267) + (0.6 \times 250) = 256.8$

1.1.12 $F_t = \alpha(A_{t-1}) + (1 - \alpha)F_{t-1} = (0.2 \times 25) + (0.8 \times 38) = 35.4$

1.1.13 $F_t = \alpha(A_{t-1}) + (1 - \alpha)F_{t-1} = (0.2 \times 30) + (0.8 \times 35.4) = 34.32$

1.1.14 $F_t = \alpha(A_{t-1}) + (1 - \alpha)F_{t-1} = (0.25 \times 4{,}075) + (0.75 \times 4{,}670) = 4{,}521.25$

1.1.15 $F_t = \alpha(A_{t-1}) + (1 - \alpha)F_{t-1} = (0.4 \times 4{,}075) + (0.6 \times 4{,}670) = 4{,}432$

1.1.16

Period	Demand	Forecast
Jan	105	76
Feb	85	84.7
Mar	80	84.79
Apr	103	83.35
May	126	89.25
Jun	145	100.28
Jul		113.7

1.1.17 Remember the following equations:

$$F_t = \alpha(A_{t-1}) + (1 - \alpha)(F_{t-1} + T_{t-1})$$

$$T_t = \beta(F_t - F_{t-1}) + (1 - \beta)T_t$$

$$FIT_t = F_t + T_t$$

Period	Actual (A)	Forecast (F)	Trend (T)	FIT
1	76	74.00	4.00	–
2	82	77.40	3.76	81.16
3	83	81.41	3.86	85.27
4	85	84.59	3.59	88.18
5	?	87.23	3.21	90.44

1.1.18

Period	Actual (A)	Forecast (F)	Trend (T)	FIT
1	76	74.00	4.00	–
2	82	77.00	3.50	80.5
3	83	81.25	3.88	85.13
4	85	84.07	3.35	87.42
5	?	86.21	2.75	88.96

1.1.19

Period	Actual (A)	Forecast (F)	Trend (T)	FIT
1	720	680	50	–
2	?	727	49.4	**776.4**

1.1.20

Period	Actual (A)	Forecast (F)	Trend (T)	FIT
1	720	680.00	50.00	–
2	830	727.00	49.40	776.4
3	?	792.48	52.62	**845.1**

1.1.21

Month	2006	2007	2008	Ave 06-08 demand	Ave monthly demand	Seasonal index	Forecast demand
Jan	10.00	10.00	15.00	11.67	44.53	0.26	13.10
Feb	15.00	12.00	15.00	14.00	44.53	0.31	15.72
Mar	15.00	20.00	17.00	17.33	44.53	0.39	19.46
Apr	20.00	18.00	25.00	21.00	44.53	0.47	23.58
May	50.00	45.00	46.00	47.00	44.53	1.06	52.78
Jun	75.00	80.00	75.00	76.67	44.53	1.72	86.09
Jul	85.00	80.00	75.00	80.00	44.53	1.80	89.83
Aug	110.00	100.00	95.00	101.67	44.53	2.28	114.16
Sep	75.00	70.00	85.00	76.67	44.53	1.72	86.09
Oct	40.00	40.00	45.00	41.67	44.53	0.94	46.79
Nov	20.00	20.00	15.00	18.33	44.53	0.41	20.59
Dec	30.00	25.00	30.00	28.33	44.53	0.64	31.82
Total average annual demand				534.33			

1.1.22

Month	2006	2007	2008	Ave 06-08 demand	Ave monthly demand	Seasonal index	Forecast demand
Jan	300.00	250.00	275.00	275.00	554.17	0.50	310.15
Feb	200.00	250.00	225.00	225.00	554.17	0.41	253.76
Mar	500.00	550.00	600.00	550.00	554.17	0.99	620.30
Apr	750.00	700.00	600.00	683.33	554.17	1.23	770.67
May	600.00	500.00	450.00	516.67	554.17	0.93	582.70
Jun	900.00	850.00	800.00	850.00	554.17	1.53	958.64
Jul	1,100.00	900.00	1,200.00	1,066.67	554.17	1.92	1,203.00
Aug	950.00	900.00	800.00	883.33	554.17	1.59	996.23
Sep	600.00	550.00	625.00	591.67	554.17	1.07	667.29
Oct	300.00	300.00	350.00	316.67	554.17	0.57	357.14
Nov	250.00	225.00	250.00	241.67	554.17	0.44	272.55
Dec	400.00	450.00	500.00	450.00	554.17	0.81	507.52
Total average annual demand				6,650.00			

1.1.23 $y^{>} = a + bx$ $y^{8} = 256.0 + (6.7 \times 8) = 309.6$

1.1.24

Year	Time period (x)	Demand (y)	x^2	xy
2003	1	500	1	500
2004	2	650	4	1,300
2005	3	700	9	2,100
2006	4	725	16	2,900
2007	5	810	25	4,050
2008	6	820	36	4,920
	$\sum x = 21$	$\sum y = 4{,}205$	$\sum x^2 = 91$	$\sum xy = 15{,}770$

Using the equations, we can calculate $\bar{x}$, $\bar{y}$, b, a and $y^>$:

$$\bar{x} = \frac{\sum x}{n} = \frac{21}{6} = 3.5$$

$$\bar{y} = \frac{\sum y}{n} = \frac{4{,}205}{6} = 700.83$$

$$b = \frac{\sum xy - n\bar{x}\bar{y}}{\sum x^2 - n\left(\bar{x}^2\right)} = \frac{15{,}770 - (6)(3.5)(700.83)}{91 - (6)(3.5^2)} = \frac{1{,}052.50}{17.50} = 60.14$$

$$a = \bar{y} - b\bar{x} = 700.83 - (60.14 \times 3.50) = 490.34$$

Therefore, the least squares trend equations is:

$$y^> = a + bx = 490.34 + 60.14x$$

Therefore, demand for 2009 (period 7) is forecast as:

$$y^{2009} = 490.34 + (60.14 \times 7) = 911.32$$

1.1.25 The least squares trend equations is: $y^> = a + bx = 490.34 + 60.14x$

Therefore, demand for 2012 (period 10) is forecast as:

$$y^{2012} = 490.34 + (60.14 \times 10) = 1{,}091.74$$

1.1.26

Year	Time period (x)	Demand (y)	x^2	xy
2003	1	56	1	56
2004	2	67	4	134
2005	3	80	9	240
2006	4	87	16	348
2007	5	80	25	400
2008	6	98	36	588
	$\sum x = 21$	$\sum y = 468$	$\sum x^2 = 91$	$\sum xy = 1{,}766$

Using the equations, we can calculate $\bar{x}$, $\bar{y}$, b, a and $y^>$:

$$\bar{x} = \frac{\sum x}{n} = \frac{21}{6} = 3.5$$

$$\bar{y} = \frac{\sum y}{n} = \frac{468}{6} = 78.00$$

$$b = \frac{\sum xy - n\bar{x}\bar{y}}{\sum x^2 - n(\bar{x}^2)} = \frac{1{,}766 - (6)(3.5)(78.0)}{91 - (6)(3.5^2)} = \frac{128}{17.50} = 7.31$$

$$a = \bar{y} - b\bar{x} = 78.00 - (7.31 \times 3.50) = 52.42$$

Therefore, the least squares trend equations is: $y^> = 52.42 + 7.31x$

Therefore, demand for 2015 (period 13) is forecast as:

$$y^{2015} = 52.42 + (7.31 \times 13) = 147.45$$

1.1.27

Year	Time period (x)	Demand (y)	x^2	xy
2003	1	56	1	56
2004	2	67	4	134
2005	3	80	9	240
2006	4	87	16	348
2007	5	80	25	400
2008	6	98	36	588
2009	7	120	49	840
	$\sum x = 28$	$\sum y = 588$	$\sum x^2 = 140$	$\sum xy = 2{,}606$

Using the equations, we can calculate $\bar{x}$, $\bar{y}$, b, a and $y^>$:

$$\bar{x} = \frac{\sum x}{n} = \frac{28}{7} = 4.0$$

$$\bar{y} = \frac{\sum y}{n} = \frac{588}{7} = 84.0$$

$$b = \frac{\sum xy - n\bar{x}\bar{y}}{\sum x^2 - n(\bar{x}^2)} = \frac{2606 - (7)(4.0)(84.0)}{140 - (7)(4.0^2)} = \frac{254}{28.0} = 9.07$$

$$a = \bar{y} - b\bar{x} = 84.0 - (9.07 \times 4.0) = 47.72$$

Therefore, the least squares trend equations is:
$$y^> = 47.72 + 9.07x$$

Therefore, the new demand forecast for 2015 (period 13) is:

$$y^{2015} = 47.72 + (9.07 \times 13) = 165.63$$

1.2 Associative forecasting

1.2.1 $y^> = 11.68 + 0.85x$

$y^{\text{€33million}} = 11.68 + (0.85 \times 33) = 39.73$ or 3,973,000 'all clears'

1.2.2 $y^{\text{€45million}} = 11.68 + (0.85 \times 45) = 49.93$ or 4,993,000 'all clears'

1.2.3

Independent (x)	Dependent (y)	x^2	xy
30	203	900	6,090
35	225	1,225	7,875
50	334	2,500	16,700
56	350	3,136	19,600
60	413	3,600	24,780
75	551	5,625	41,325
306	2,076	16,986	116,370

$$\sum x = 306 \qquad \sum y - 2,076 \qquad \sum x^2 = 16,986 \qquad \sum xy = 116,370$$

$$\bar{x} = \frac{\sum x}{n} = \frac{306}{6} = 51$$

$$\bar{y} = \frac{\sum y}{n} = \frac{2,076}{6} = 346$$

$$b = \frac{\sum xy - n\bar{x}\bar{y}}{\sum x^2 - n\left(\bar{x}^2\right)} = \frac{116,370 - (6)(51)(346)}{16,986 - (6)(51^2)} = \frac{10,494}{1,380} = 7.604$$

$$a = \bar{y} - b\bar{x} = 346 - (7.604 \times 51) = -41.804$$

Therefore, the least squares trend equations is:

$y^> = -41.804 + 7.604x$

$y^{\text{€90,000marketing}} = -41.804 + (7.604 \times 90) = 642.556$ or €642,556

1.2.4

Independent (x)	Dependent (y)	x^2	xy
15	145	225	2,175
20	130	400	2,600
22	120	484	2,640
25	100	625	2,500
26	105	676	2,730
30	90	900	2,700
138	690	3,310	15,345
$\sum x = 138$	$\sum y = 690$	$\sum x^2 = 3{,}310$	$\sum xy = 15{,}345$

$$\bar{x} = \frac{\sum x}{n} = \frac{138}{6} = 23$$

$$\bar{y} = \frac{\sum y}{n} = \frac{690}{6} = 115$$

$$b = \frac{\sum xy - n\bar{x}\,\bar{y}}{\sum x^2 - n\left(\bar{x}^2\right)} = \frac{15{,}345 - (6)\,(23)\,(115)}{3{,}310 - (6)\,(23^2)} = \frac{-525}{136} = -3.860$$

$$a = \bar{y} - b\bar{x} = 115 - (-3.860 \times 23) = 203.787$$

Therefore, the least squares trend equations is:

$$y^> = 203.787 + (-3.860)(x)$$

$$y^{35 instructors} = 203.787 + (-3.860)(35) = 68.68 \text{ accidents}$$

1.2.5 $\sum x = 405 \qquad \sum y = 259 \qquad \sum x^2 = 32{,}975 \qquad \sum xy = 21{,}105$

Least squares trend equations is $y^> = -8.235 + 0.741x$

$$y^{\$120 per person} = -8.235 + (0.741 \times 120) = 80.71\% \text{ compliance}$$

1.3   Forecast error

1.3.1 $MAD = \dfrac{\sum |E_t|}{n} = \dfrac{24}{4} = 6$

1.3.2 $MAD = \dfrac{\sum |E_t|}{n} = \dfrac{80}{5} = 16$

1.3.3 $MAD = \dfrac{\sum |E_t|}{n} = \dfrac{44}{6} = 7.33 \qquad MSE = \dfrac{\sum E_t^2}{n} = \dfrac{478}{6} = 79.67$

1.3.4 $MAD = 2.6$ $MSE = 7.8$ $MAPE = 10.93$

1.3.5 $MAD = 22.54$ $MSE = 766.92$ $MAPE = 18.84$

1.3.6 (a) Smoothed forecast

Month	Actual sales	New forecast ($\alpha = 0.5$)
Jan	105	76.00
Feb	85	90.50
Mar	80	87.75
Apr	103	83.88
May	126	93.44
Jun	145	109.72

(b) $MAD = 3.23$ $MSE = 587.82$ $MAPE = 18.23$

(c) The new forecast is better because all measures of forecast error are lower.

Chapter 2 Descriptive techniques

2.1 EBIT and NPV

2.1.1 From €180,000 to €227,000 = 26.1%

2.1.2 The radio campaign should result in a 30.9% increase in sales from €805,000 to €1,053,745. Costs will rise from €578,000 to €778,000. Therefore, the expected EBIT resulting from the second radio campaign is €275,745.

2.1.3 Investing in the automated bread machines should reduce total operating costs by 30% from €638,000 (€578,000 + €60,000 investment) to €446,600. Therefore, expected EBIT would be €358,400, which is significantly higher than the EBIT of investing in a second radio campaign.

2.1.4 $P = FX = 30,000 \times 0.596 = \$17,880$

2.1.5 $P = FX = 250,000 \times 0.481 = £120,250$

2.1.6 $S = RX = 40,000 \times 3.890 = \$155,600$

2.1.7 $S = RX = 55,000 \times 3.433 = \$188,815 - \$130,000$ (initial investment)
$= \$58,815$

2.1.8   Machine A is the low-cost purchase

	Machine A			Machine B		
Year	Expense	Discount (12%)	NPV	Expense	Discount (12%)	NPV
0	35,000	1.00	35,000	42,000	1.00	42,000
1	12,700	0.893	11,341	12,600	0.893	11,252
2	12,700	0.797	10,122	12,600	0.797	10,042
3	12,700	0.712	9,042	12,600	0.712	8,971
4	12,700	0.636	8,077	12,600	0.636	8,014
	(3,000) scrap	0.636	(1,908)	(4,900)	0.636	3,116
		Total	71,674		Total	77,163

2.1.9

Year	Cash flow	Table factor (7%)	Present value
0	(680,000)	1.000	(680,000)
1	235,000	0.935	219,725
2	290,000	0.873	253,170
3	290,000	0.816	236,640
4	250,000	0.763	190,750
		NPV	£220,285

2.1.10

Year	Cash flow	Table factor (14%)	Present value
0	(850,000)	1.000	(850,000)
1	235,000	.877	206,095
2	290,000	.769	223,010
3	290,000	.675	195,750
4	250,000	.592	148,000
		NPV	(£77,145)

2.1.11

Year	Cash flow	Table factor (4%)	Present value
0	(0)	1.000	(0)
1	$(400 \times 80) - (4000 + (400 \times 5)) = 29,600$	0.962	28,475.20
2	$(500 \times 80) - (4000 + (500 \times 5)) = 33,500$	0.925	30,987.50
3	$(600 \times 80) - (4000 + (600 \times 5)) = 41,000$	0.889	36,449.00
4	$(600 \times 80) - (4000 + (600 \times 5)) = 41,000$	0.855	35,055.00
		NPV	€130,966.70

2.2 Productivity and efficiency

2.2.1   Labour productivity (orders per hour) $= \dfrac{8,750}{550} = 15.91$ orders/hr

Labour productivity (sales value per hour) $=$

$$\frac{(350 \times \$5)(8,400 \times \$25)}{550} = \$385/hr$$

2.2.2   (a) Old system: 12.86 invoices per hour.
New system: 32.14 invoices per hour.

    (b) Labour productivity has risen significantly. The change is 32.14 / 12.86 = 2.49, a 250% increase in labour productivity.

    (c) Old system: .69 invoices per pound.
New system: .67 invoices per pound.

    (d) Multi-factor productivity has slightly decreased. The change is .69 / .67 = .97, a 3% reduction.

2.2.3   (a) Current labour productivity $= \dfrac{12 \times 1,400}{100 \times 6} = \dfrac{16,800}{600} = 28$ meals per labour hour

    (b) New labour productivity $= \dfrac{16 \times 1,400}{100 \times 6} = \dfrac{22,400}{600} = 37.3$ meals per labour hour

    (c) Current multi-factor productivity $= \dfrac{16,800}{700,000} = 0.024$ meals per yen

    (d) New multi-factor productivity $= \dfrac{22,400}{1,200,000} = 0.019$ meals per yen

    (e) Whilst labour productivity would increase by 33% if the equipment were purchased, the increase in production is outweighed by the additional costs. As the multi-factor productivity would fall from 0.024 to 0.019 meals per yen (21%), this investment is not justifiable.

2.2.4   Throughput efficiency = 0.075 or 7.5%

2.2.5   Throughput efficiency = 0.1 or 10%

2.2.6   *VATE* = 0.07 or 7%

2.2.7   Throughput efficiency = 0.333 or 33.3%
VATE = 0.222 or 22.2%

2.2.8   Throughput time = 1080 minutes
Throughput efficiency = 0.046 or 4.6%

2.3 Capacity and requirements calculation

2.3.1 $(6 \times 1.5) + (5 \times 2) + (3 \times 3) = 9 + 10 + 9 = 28 \min$

The number of units that can be produced per week is:

$$\frac{700 \times 60}{28} \times 14 = 21,000 \text{ units}$$

2.3.2 $(2 \times 1.5) + (3 \times 2) + (7 \times 3) = 3 + 6 + 21 = 30\,\text{min}$

The number of units that can be produced per week is:

$$\frac{700 \times 60}{30} \times 14 = 19,600 \text{ units}$$

2.3.3 80%

2.3.4 $2,460 \times 0.82 = 2,017.2$

2.3.5 (a) Document checking = 121,600; Licence production = 135,000; Distribution = 120,000

(b) Document checking = 121,000/145,000 = 83.9%

Licence production = 135,000/1,250,000 = 10.8%

Distribution = 120,000/165,000 = 72.7%

2.3.6 Actual production was $\left(\frac{36,000}{96}\right) \times (96 - 60) = 13,500$

Effective capacity = 96 − 33 = 63 hours

$$\text{Utilisation} = \frac{Actual\ output}{Design\ capacity} = \frac{36}{96} = 0.375\,(37.5\%)$$

$$\text{Efficiency} = \frac{Actual\ output}{Effective\ capacity} = \frac{36}{63} = 0.571\,(57.1\%)$$

2.3.7 New production $\left(\frac{36,000}{96}\right) \times (96 - 36) = 22,500$

Effective capacity = 96 − 21 = 75 hours

$$\text{Utilisation} = \frac{Actual\ output}{Design\ capacity} = \frac{60}{96} = 0.625\,(62.5\%)$$

$$\text{Efficiency} = \frac{Actual\ output}{Effective\ capacity} = \frac{60}{75} = 0.8\,(80.0\%)$$

2.3.8 Loading time = 152 hours

Availability losses = (2 hours not worked unplanned) + (9 hours set-up) + (3 hours breakdown)

So, total operating time = 152 − 14 = 138 hours

Speed losses = (4 hours idling) + ((138 − 4) × 0.11 slow running) = 4 + 14.74 = 18.74 hours

So, net operating time = 138 − 18.74 = 119.21 hours

Quality losses = (119.21 net operating time) × (0.04 error rate) = 4.7 hours

So, valuable operating time = 119.21 − 4.7 = 114.56 hours

$$\text{Availability rate} = \frac{\textit{Total operating time}}{\textit{Loading time}} = \frac{138}{152} = 0.9079 = 90.79\%$$

$$\text{Performance rate} = \frac{\textit{Net operating time}}{\textit{Total operating time}} = \frac{119.26}{138} = 0.8642 = 86.42\%$$

$$\text{Quality rate} = \frac{\textit{Valuable operating time}}{\textit{Net operating time}} = \frac{114.56}{119.26} = 0.9606 = 96.06\%$$

$$OEE = a \times p \times q = 0.9079 \times 0.8642 \times 0.9606 = 0.7537 = 75.37\%$$

2.3.9

Loading time	152.00
not worked (unplanned)	2.00
set-up changeover	6.00
breakdown failure	1.00
Total operating time	**143.00**
Equipment 'idling'	4.00
Slow running equipment	8.34
Net operating time	**130.66**
Quality losses	5.23
Valuable operating time	**125.43**
Availability rate (a)	0.94
Performance rate (p)	0.91
Quality rate (q)	0.96
OEE ($a \times p \times q$)	0.83

2.3.10

Loading time	48.00
not worked (unplanned)	1.00
set-up changeover	0.50
breakdown failure	1.50
Total operating time	**45.00**
Equipment 'idling'	0.75
Slow running equipment	9.74
Net operating time	**34.52**
Quality losses	5.18
Valuable operating time	**29.34**
Availability rate (a)	0.94
Performance rate (p)	0.77
Quality rate (q)	0.85
OEE ($a \times p \times q$)	0.61

2.3.11 $M = \dfrac{Dp}{N[1 - (C / 100)]} = \dfrac{14{,}000{,}000 \times 0.005}{(22 \times 360)\,[1 - (7 / 100)]}$

$\qquad = \dfrac{70{,}000}{7{,}920 \times 0.93} = 9.50$

Rounding up to the next integer gives a machine requirement of 10.

2.3.12

Process hours required for annual demand	75,000.000
Hours available from one machine/server – desired cushion	7,161.000
(*M*) Machines	10.473

2.3.13

Process hours required for annual demand	6,000.000
Hours available from one machine/server – desired cushion	1,632.000
(*M*) Servers required	3.676

2.3.14 Accounts required (*M*)

$$M = \frac{[Dp + (D/Q)s]simple + [Dp + (D/Q)s]complex + \cdots + [Dp + (D/Q)s]product\,n}{N[1 - (C/100)]}$$

$$= \frac{[6{,}500(0.7) + (6{,}500/8)0.05]Simple + [2{,}500(1.5) + (2{,}500/5)0.05]Complex}{1{,}920[1 - (10/100)]}$$

$$= \frac{4{,}590.63 + 3{,}775}{1{,}920 \times 0.9} = \frac{8{,}365.63}{1{,}728} = 4.84$$

… so the firm currently has enough accounts to meet demand.

2.3.15 5.54 accounts are required – round up to 6.

2.3.16 11.85 machines required – round up to 12.

2.3.17

Total process hours required for annual demand	2,490.50
(N) Total processing hours per annum	900.00
(C) Capacity cushion	12.00%
Hours available from one surgeon – desired cushion	792.00
(M) Surgeons required	3.14

2.4 Work measurement

2.4.1 9.533 minutes

2.4.2 8.471 minutes

2.4.3 4.167 minutes

2.4.4

	Ave time	Basic time	Standard time
Fabric cutting	11.000	13.20	14.67
Stitching	17.000	15.30	17.00
Packaging	2.250	1.91	2.13
Total standard time	**33.792**		

2.4.5

	Ave time	Basic time	Standard time
Empty bins	0.950	0.86	1.01
Vacuum floor	3.714	4.64	5.46
Total standard time	**6.468**		

2.4.6 $z = 2.56$ $s = 155.00$ $h = 0.05$ $\bar{x} = 500.00$

2.4.7 *Required sample size* $= n = \left(\dfrac{zs}{h\bar{x}}\right)^2 = \left(\dfrac{2.58 \times 155}{0.05 \times 500}\right)^2 = 255.87 \approx 256$

2.4.8 *Required sample size* $= n = \left(\dfrac{zs}{h\bar{x}}\right)^2 = \left(\dfrac{1.65 \times 0.8}{0.1 \times 1.8}\right)^2 = 53.78 \approx 54$

$n = 135.24$

2.4.9 First, we solve for the mean $\bar{x}$ and for standard deviation s.

$\bar{x} = 2.80$

$$s = \sqrt{\dfrac{\sum(each\ sample\ observation\ -\ \bar{x})^2}{number\ in\ sample\ -\ 1}}$$

Observation	Time (x_i)	x-	$x_i - x-$	$(x_i - x-)^2$
1	2.60	2.80	−0.20	0.04
2	2.90	2.80	0.10	0.01
3	2.20	2.80	−0.60	0.36
4	3.00	2.80	0.20	0.04
5	3.30	2.80	0.50	0.25
				0.7

$s = \sqrt{\dfrac{0.7}{4}} = 0.418$

Now we can solve for $n = \left(\dfrac{zs}{h\bar{x}}\right)^2 = \left(\dfrac{2.58 \times 0.418}{0.04 \times 2.80}\right)^2 = 92.86 \approx 93$

2.4.10 $n = \dfrac{z^2 p(1 - p)}{h^2} = \dfrac{(2.58)^2(0.25)(0.75)}{(0.1)^2} = 124.81 \approx 125$

2.4.11 $499.23 \approx 500$

2.4.12 $385.69 \approx 386$

2.4.13 No, it needs to be $80.67 \approx 81$

2.5 Failure, reliability and redundancy

2.5.1 $FR^{\%} = \dfrac{Number\ of\ failures}{Total\ number\ of\ products\ tested} \times 100 = \dfrac{21}{2,800} = 0.75\%$

2.5.2 $FR^{\%} = 1.25\%$ $FR^{time} = 0.0000025\ per\ hour$

2.5.3 $FR^{\%} = 4.0\%$ Non-operating time = 865 hours

$$MTBF = \dfrac{1}{number\ of\ failures} = \dfrac{1}{0.000027}$$
$$= 37,037.04\ \text{hours between failures}$$

2.5.4 (a) 14.29%

(b) 1,455 hours

(c) 0.00019 per hour

(d) 5,263.16 hours

2.5.5 (a) 6.67%

(b) 1,315 hours

(c) 0.000057

(d) 17,543.86 hours

2.5.6 (a) 0.763

(b) 0.99

(c) 0.839

2.5.7 (a) 0.747

(b) 0.988

(c) 0.831

2.5.8 The reliability of components R_1 and R_2 and R_3 working in parallel, R_{1+2+3}, is calculated as:

$$R_{1+2+3} = R_1 + \left[(R_2) \times (1 - R_1)\right] + \left[(R_3) \times (1 - R_{1+2})\right]$$

$$R_{1+2+3} = 0.90 + \left[(0.95) \times (1 - 0.90)\right] + \left[(0.85) \times (1 - 0.995)\right]$$
$$= 0.90 + 0.095 + 0.00425 = .9925$$

2.5.9 $Availability\ (A) = \dfrac{MTBF}{MTBF + MTTR} = \dfrac{24}{24 + 3} = 0.889$

2.5.10 $Availability^{preventative} = \dfrac{MTBF}{MTBF + MTTR} = \dfrac{28}{28 + 3} = 0.903$

$Availability^{fast\ repair} = \dfrac{MTBF}{MTBF + MTTR} = \dfrac{24}{24 + 2} = 0.923$

2.5.11 0.889

2.5.12 $Availability^{preventative} = 0.917$ $\qquad$ $Availability^{staff\ repair} = 0.914$

2.6 Statistical process control

2.6.1 p-chart control limits ($z = \pm 3\sigma$):

$$\sigma_p = \sqrt{\dfrac{\bar{p}(1 - \bar{p})}{n}} = \sqrt{\dfrac{0.012(1 - 0.012)}{1000}} = 0.0034$$

$$\mathrm{UCL}_p = \bar{p} + z\sigma_p = 0.012 + (3 \times 0.0034) = 0.022$$

$$\mathrm{LCL}_p = \bar{p} - z\sigma_p = 0.012 - (3 \times 0.0034) = 0.0018$$

c-chart control limits ($z = \pm 3\sigma$) can be calculated as follows:

$$\sigma_c = \sqrt{\bar{c}} = \sqrt{12.33} = 3.511$$

$$\mathrm{UCL}_c = \bar{c} + 3\sigma_c = 12.33 + (3 \times 3.511) = 22.863$$

$$\mathrm{LCL}_c = \bar{c} - 3\sigma_c = 12.33 - (3 \times 3.511) = 1.797$$

2.6.2 p-chart control limits ($z = \pm 3\sigma$):
$\mathrm{UCL}_p = 0.208$ $\qquad$ $\mathrm{LCL}_p = -0.032 = 0$

c-chart control limits ($z = \pm 3\sigma$):
$\mathrm{UCL}_c = 10.693$ $\qquad$ $\mathrm{LCL}_c = -1.893 = 0$

2.6.3 c-chart control limits ($z = \pm 3\sigma$):
$\mathrm{UCL}_c = 11.708$ $\qquad$ $\mathrm{LCL}_c = -1.708 = 0$

2.6.4 c-chart control limits ($z = \pm 3\sigma$):
$\mathrm{UCL}_c = 23.817$ $\qquad$ $\mathrm{LCL}_c = 2.183$

2.6.5 p-chart control limits ($z = \pm 3\sigma$):
$\mathrm{UCL}_p = 0.079$ $\qquad$ $\mathrm{LCL}_p = 0.021$

2.6.6 $\mathrm{UCL}_p = 0.0856 = 8.56\%$

2.6.7 $\mathrm{UCL} = D_4 \bar{R} = 1.864 \times 3.4 = 6.34$

$\mathrm{LCL} = D_3 \bar{R} = 0.136 \times 3.4 = 0.46$

2.6.8 (a) $\overline{\overline{X}} = 12.0$ $\overline{R} = 5.0$

(b) $\text{UCL} = \overline{\overline{X}} + A_2\overline{R} = 12.0 + (0.180 \times 5.0) = 12.90$

   $\text{LCL} = \overline{\overline{X}} - A_2\overline{R} = 12.0 - (0.180 \times 5.0) = 11.10$

(c) $\text{UCL} = D_4\overline{R} = 1.586 \times 5 = 7.93$

   $\text{LCL} = D_3\overline{R} = 0.414 \times 5.0 = 2.07$

2.6.9 (a) $\text{UCL} = \overline{\overline{X}} + A_2\overline{R} = 19.5 + (0.266 \times 6.0) = 21.096$

   $\text{LCL} = \overline{\overline{X}} - A_2\overline{R} = 19.5 - (0.266 \times 6.0) = 17.904$

(b) $\text{UCL} = D_4\overline{R} = 1.716 \times 6.0 = 10.296$

   $\text{LCL} = D_3\overline{R} = 0.284 \times 6.0 = 1.704$

2.6.10 (a) $\text{UCL} = \overline{\overline{X}} + A_2\overline{R} = 28.83 + (0.157 \times 6.67) = 29.88$

   $\text{LCL} = \overline{\overline{X}} - A_2\overline{R} = 28.83 - (0.157 \times 6.67) = 27.79$

(b) $\text{UCL} = D_4\overline{R} = 1.548 \times 6.67 = 10.33$

   $\text{LCL} = D_3\overline{R} = 0.452 \times 6.67 = 3.01$

2.6.11 (a) $25 + 30 + 15 + 20 + 17/5 = 21.4$

(b) $48 - 15 = 33$

(c) $\overline{\overline{X}} = 24.84$ $\overline{R} = 18.4$

(d) $\text{UCL} = \overline{\overline{X}} + A_2\overline{R} = 24.84 + (0.577 \times 18.40) = 35.46$

   $\text{LCL} = \overline{\overline{X}} - A_2\overline{R} = 24.84 - (0.577 \times 18.40) = 14.22$

(e) $\text{UCL} = D_4\overline{R} = 2.115 \times 18.40 = 38.92$

   $\text{LCL} = D_3\overline{R} = 0.0 \times 18.40 = 0.0$

(f) The process is not in control because sample 4's time average ($\overline{X}$) of 36.40 is above the upper control limit of 35.46.

2.6.12 $C_p = \dfrac{UTL - LTL}{6s} = \dfrac{25 - 10}{6 \times 5} = 0.5$ $C_{pk} = \min\left(C_{pu}, C_{pl}\right) = 0.33$

Both the capability ratio and capability index are less than 1, so this process is not capable.

2.6.13 $C_{pk} = \min\left(C_{pu}, C_{pl}\right) = (4.0, 1.33) = 1.33$

2.6.14 $C_{pk} = \min\left(C_{pu}, C_{pl}\right) = (4.67, 0.67) = 0.67$

2.6.15 $C_{pu} = 0.89$ $C_{pl} = 0.44$

2.6.16 $C_{pk} = \min\left(C_{pu}, C_{pl}\right) = (1.0, 1.0) = 1.0$

2.7 Little's Law and balancing loss

2.7.1   Cycle time $= \dfrac{Work\ content}{Number\ of\ servers} = \dfrac{4}{3} = 1.33\,\text{min}$

       $WIP = \dfrac{Throughput\ time}{Cycle\ time} = \dfrac{10\ hrs}{1.33} = 451\,\text{customers}$

2.7.2   750 customers

2.7.3   720 customers

2.7.4   1.6 minutes

2.7.5 $15.625 \approx 16$ people are needed

2.7.6   115.38, therefore 115 applications

2.7.7   48 minutes

2.7.8   66 minutes

2.7.9   112 minutes

2.7.10   Cycle time = 20 minutes

       Idle time every cycle $= (20 - 15) + (20 - 18) + (20 - 20) + (20 - 13)$
                                 $= 14$ minutes

       Balancing loss $= 14/(20 \times 4) = 0.175 = 17.5\%$

2.7.11   Idle time every cycle $= (22 - 10) + (22 - 16) + (22 - 22) +$
       $(22 - 8) + (22 - 12) = 31$ minutes

       Balancing loss $= 31/(22 \times 5) = 0.282 = 28.2\%$

2.7.12
Idle time every cycle $= (26 - 26) + (26 - 22) + (26 - 20) = 10$ minutes
Balancing loss $= 10/(26 \times 3) = 0.128 = 12.8\%$

2.8 Queuing methods

2.8.1 Utilisation of distribution counter, $u = \dfrac{18}{(8.57 \times 4)} = 0.52$

Waiting time in queue, $W_q = \dfrac{0.52^{\sqrt{2(4+1)}-1}}{4(1-0.52)} \times 0.12$

$$= 0.015 \text{ hours} = 0.9 \text{ minutes}$$

Average number of people in queue, $WIP_q = 18 \times 0.015$

$$= 0.27$$

2.8.2 Utilisation of distribution counter, $u = \dfrac{30}{(8.57 \times 4)} = 0.87$

Waiting time in queue, $W_q = \dfrac{0.87^{\sqrt{2(4+1)}-1}}{4(1-0.87)} \times 0.12$

$$= 0.17 \text{ hours}$$

$$= 10.2 \text{ minutes}$$

Average number of people in queue, $WIP_q = 30 \times 0.17$

$$= 5.1$$

Therefore the waiting time in queue would be increased from 0.9 minutes to 10.2 minutes and the average number of people in queue would also be increased from 0.27 to 5.1.

2.8.3 Utilisation of distribution counter, $u = \dfrac{18}{(8.57 \times 3)} = 0.70$

Waiting time in queue, $W_q = \dfrac{0.7^{\sqrt{2(3+1)}-1}}{3(1-0.7)} \times 0.12$

$$= 0.069 \text{ hours}$$

$$= 4.18 \text{ minutes}$$

2.8.4 Utilisation of the single service counter, $u = 8/10 = 0.8$

Waiting time in queue, $W_q = \dfrac{0.8}{(1-0.8)} \times 0.1$

$$= 0.4 \text{ hours}$$

$$= 24 \text{ minutes}$$

Average number of customers, $WIP_q = \dfrac{0.8^2}{1-0.8} = 3.2$

2.8.5 Processing time per customer, $t_e = \dfrac{5 \times (1 - 0.8}{0.8}$

$$= 1.25 \text{ minutes}$$

2.8.6 Processing rate $= 10/0.9 = 11.11$ per hour

2.8.7 Utilisation of check – in counter, $u = \dfrac{10}{(6 \times 4)} = 0.42$

Average waiting time in queue,

$$W_q = \left(\frac{1.5^2 + 3.5^2}{2} \right) \left(\frac{0.42^{\sqrt{2(4+1)}-1}}{4(1-0.42)} \right) \times 0.17$$

$$= 0.08 \text{ hours}$$

$$= 4.8 \text{ minutes}$$

2.8.8 Average waiting time in queue,

$$W_q = \left(\frac{1.5^2 + 2.5^2}{2} \right) \left(\frac{0.42^{\sqrt{2(4+1)}-1}}{4(1-0.42)} \right) \times 0.17$$

$$= 0.047 \text{ hours}$$

$$= 2.28 \text{ minutes}$$

After reducing the coefficient of variation of processing time, the waiting time in queue would also be decreased from 4.8 minutes to 2.28 minutes.

2.8.9 Average waiting time in queue,

$$W_q = \left(\frac{2.0^2 + 3.0^2}{2} \right) \left(\frac{0.42^{\sqrt{2(4+1)}-1}}{4(1-0.42)} \right) \times 0.17$$

$$= 0.07 \text{ hours}$$

$$= 4.2 \text{ minutes}$$

After changing the coefficient of variation of arrival time and processing time, the waiting time in queue would be decreased from 4.8 minutes to 4.2 minutes.

2.8.10 Utilisation of the ticket counter, $u = \dfrac{15}{20} = 0.75$

$$\text{Waiting time in queue, } W_q = \left(\frac{1^2 + 3^2}{2}\right)\left(\frac{0.75}{(1-0.75)}\right) \times 0.05$$

$$= \quad 0.75 \text{ hours}$$

$$= \quad 45 \text{ minutes}$$

$$\text{Average number of passengers in queue, } WIP_q = 15 \times 0.75$$

$$= 11.25$$

2.8.11 $\text{Waiting time in queue, } W_q = \left(\frac{1^2 + 1.5^2}{2}\right)\left(\frac{0.75}{(1-0.75)}\right) \times 0.05$

$$= \quad 0.24 \text{ hours}$$

$$= \quad 14.4 \text{ minutes}$$

$$\text{Average number of passengers in queue, } WIP_q = 15 \times 0.24$$

$$= 3.6$$

After reducing the coefficient of variation of processing time, the average number of passengers in queue would also be decreased from 11.25 to 3.6.

2.8.12 $\text{Waiting time in queue, } W_q = \left(\frac{1.5^2 + 2.5^2}{2}\right)\left(\frac{0.75}{(1-0.75)}\right) \times 0.05$

$$= \quad 0.64 \text{ hours}$$

$$= \quad 38.4 \text{ minutes}$$

$$\text{Average number of passengers in queue, } WIP_q = 15 \times 0.64$$

$$= 9.6$$

After changing the coefficient of variation of arrival time and processing time, the number of passengers in queue has decreased from 11.25 to 9.6.

Chapter 3 Evaluative techniques

3.1 Break-even analysis

3.1.1 Break-even in units $= \dfrac{F}{P - V} = \dfrac{3,250}{5.95 - 2.50} = 942$ bottles per month

3.1.2 Break-even in units $= \dfrac{F}{P - V} = \dfrac{4,200}{5.95 - 1.25} = 893.6$ bottles per month

Break-even in pounds $= \dfrac{F}{1 - (V / P)} = \dfrac{4,200}{1 - [(1.25) / (5.95)]}$

$= \dfrac{4,200}{0.7899} = £5,317$

3.1.3 Break-even in pounds $= \dfrac{F}{1 - (V / P)} = \dfrac{750,000}{1 - [(975) / (2,450)]}$

$= \dfrac{750,000}{0.602} = £1,245,847$

3.1.4 Break-even in units $= \dfrac{F}{P - V} = \dfrac{265,000}{120 - (30 + 22)} = 3,897$ cakes per year are needed to break even, but the firm only expects to sell 3,000 cakes each year, so they will not break even.

3.1.5 Reducing fixed costs (option A) brings the break-even point down by more than reducing variable costs (option B) and is therefore preferable.

Option A: Break-even in units $= \dfrac{F}{P - V} = \dfrac{175,000}{120 - (30 + 22)} = 2,573.5$ cakes per year

Option B: Break-even in units $= \dfrac{F}{P - V} = \dfrac{265,000}{120 - (15 + 22)} = 3,192.8$ cakes per year

3.1.6 Before we can proceed with break-even analysis, we must weight each of the items by its proportion of total sales.

1	2	3	4	5	6	7	8
Item (*i*)	Price (*P*)	Variable cost (*V*)	(*V*/*P*)	1 − (*V*/*P*)	Annual revenue (€)	Proportion of sales revenue	Weighted contribution (col. 5 × col. 7)
Margherita	6.00	2.00	.33	.67	45,000	.16	.107
Napoli	7.50	2.50	.33	.67	37,500	.13	.087
Americano	7.50	2.75	.36	.64	48,750	.17	.109
Quattro Formaggi	8.50	3.00	.35	.65	72,250	.26	.169
Tropicano	8.00	3.00	.38	.62	32,000	.12	.074
Funghi	7.00	2.25	.32	.68	45,500	.16	.109
Total					281,000	1.00	.655

Using this approach for each item, we find the total weighted contribution is .655 for each euro of sales, and the break-even point is €25,954.

$$BEP_\epsilon = \frac{F}{\sum\left[\left(1 - \frac{V_i}{P_i}\right) \times (W_i)\right]} = \frac{17,000}{.655} = €25,954$$

3.1.7 Daily sales required $= \dfrac{Annual\ sales}{Operating\ days} = \dfrac{25,954}{250} = €103.81$

3.1.8 Total annual profit = Total revenue – (Fixed costs + Variable costs)

$= 281,000 - [17,000$

$\qquad + \sum[(7,500 \times 2) + (5,000 \times 2.5) + (6,500 \times 2.75) + (8,500 \times 3)$

$\qquad + (4,000 \times 3) + (6,500 \times 2.25)] = 281,000 - (17,000 + 97,500)$

$= €166,500$ annual profit

3.1.9 $BEP_x = \dfrac{F_a - F_b}{V_b - V_a} = \dfrac{245,000 - 135,000}{4.15 - 3.50} = 169,230.7$

$\qquad \approx 169,231$ garments

If sales are forecast to exceed 169,231 garments in the time period, then machine *a* is the better investment.

3.1.10 New $BEP_x = \dfrac{F_a - F_b}{V_b - V_a} = \dfrac{200,000 - 135,000}{4.35 - 3.50} = 76,470.6$

$\qquad \approx 76,471$ garments

The reduction in fixed cost of machine *a* and the increase in variable cost of machine *b* means that only 76,471 garments need to be produced for machine *a* to be the better investment.

3.1.11 $BEP_x = \dfrac{F_c - F_a}{V_a - V_c} = \dfrac{450,000 - 200,000}{3.50 - 1.65} = 135,135.13$

$\qquad \approx 135,136$ garments

In this case, Axon should invest in the machine *c* because the point at which it is preferable to adopt this option is lower than the forecast demand.

Machine *a* total costs = F + V

$= 200,000 + (3.5 \times 240,000) = \$1,040,000$

Machine *b* total costs = F + V

$= 450,000 + (1.65 \times 240,000) = \$846,000$

3.2 Weighted score method

3.2.1

		Weighted score (score × weight)	
Critical success factors	Weight	Upgrade online accounts	Personal banking
Market potential	.35	29.75	26.25
Labour skills	.15	12	7.5
Unit profit margin	.10	6	9
Operations capability	.10	6	7.5
Risk	.15	10.5	11.25
Investment required	.15	6	9
Totals	**1.00**	**70.25**	**70.5**

The personal banking for high earners appears to be a marginally better option. However, its market potential, which is most heavily weighted, is not as promising as the upgrade to online accounts.

3.2.2 The firm should not invest in the new microchip, because the weighted score is not as good as 7.35.

Performance criteria	Weight	Weighted score
Market potential	.25	1.25
Competitive advantage	.10	0.7
Unit profit margin	.30	2.4
Location of supply	.05	0.15
Risk	.10	0.5
Investment required	.20	1
Totals	**1.00**	**6.0**

3.2.3 Service A = 12 + 15 + 7 + 12 + 10 = 56

Service B = 14 + 10 + 15 + 9 + 9 = 57

Service C = 8 + 18 + 16 + 6 + 7 = 55

3.2.4 France = 56.5

Spain = 60.5

3.3 Decision theory

3.3.1 (a) *Maximin.* Order 50,000 books (€180,000 vs. €110,000)

(b) *Maximax.* Order 100,000 books (€550,000 vs. €210,000)

(c) *Laplace.* Order 100,000 books (€330,000 vs. €195,000)

(d) *Minimax regret.* Order 100,00 (Maximum regret €340,000 vs. €70,000)

3.3.2 Order 100,000 books, because it represents the best weighted profit potential.

- Expected profits of 50,000 book order = $(.65 \times 180,000) + (.35 \times 210,000) = €190,500$

- Expected profit of 100,000 book order = $(.65 \times 110,000) + (.35 \times 550,000) = €264,000$

3.3.3 The best payoff is €180,000 for low demand, €550,000 for high demand. The best expected value (*EV*) without perfect information is for the 100,000 book order, whereas for perfect information we have both best payoffs:

$$EV_{imperfect =} (0.65 \times 110,000) + (.35 \times 550,000) = €264,000$$

$$EV_{perfect =} (0.65 \times 180,000) + (.35 \times 550,000) = €309,500$$

Therefore, the value of perfect information is €309,500 – €264,000 = €45,500. If a perfect forecast is achievable, it is worth up to, but no more than, €45,500.

3.3.4

Alternative	Payoffs under different demand		
	Low (50 boxes)	Medium (100 boxes)	High (200 boxes)
Order 50	(50 × 25) – (50 × 8) = £850	(50 × 25) – (50 × 8) = £850	(50 × 25) – (50 × 8) = £850
Order 100	(50 × 25) – (100 × 8) = £450	(100 × 25) – (100 × 8) = £1,700	(100 × 25) – (100 × 8) = £1,700
Order 200	(50 × 25) – (200 × 8) = (£350)	(100 × 25) – (200 × 8) = £900	(200 × 25) – (200 × 8) = £3,400
Do nothing	0	0	0

(a) *Maximin.* Order 50 boxes – £850 profit, as opposed to £450 profit or £350 loss.

(b) *Maximax.* Order 200 boxes – £3,400 profit, as opposed £1,700 profit or £850 profit.

(c) *Laplace.* Order 200 boxes. Equally weighted payoffs for ordering 50, 100 and 200 are £850, £1,283.3, £1,316.67 respectively.

(d) *Minimax regret.* Graham should order 200 boxes. The maximum regret of ordering 50 boxes occurs if demand is high (£3,400 – £850 = £2,550). The maximum regret of ordering 100 boxes occurs if demand is high (£3,400 – £1,700 = £1,700). The maximum regret of ordering 200 boxes occurs if demand is low (£850 – (–£350) = £1,200).

3.3.5 (a) *Maximax.* Graham's more accurate forecast of demand has no effect, because the best scenario remains the 200 boxes sold at a profit of £3,400.

(b) *Expected value.* Weightings have now changed to .3, .5, .2 for the three scenarios. This means the expected value is £850, £1,325 and £1,025 respectively. Under this decision criteria, Graham should only buy 100 boxes as it represents a better weighted average.

3.3.6 Payoff table for the three options:

	Payoffs under different MOD strategies		
Alternative	'Micro engagement'	'Euro-collaboration'	'Turbo thrust'
Alpha 1	(10,000 × 200) – (450,00 + (10,000 × 60)) = £1,895,000	(5,000 × 200) – (450,00 + (5,000 × 60)) = £250,000	(20,000 × 20) – (450,000 + (20,000 × 60)) = £3,835,000
Delta 4	(5,000 × 350) – (500,000 + (5,000 × 150)) = 500,000	(15,000 × 350) – (500,000 + (15,000 × 150)) = 2,500,000	(30,000 × 350) – (500,000 + (30,000 × 150)) = 5,500,000
Gamma 7	(15,000 × 500) – (800,000 + (15,000 × 250)) = 2,950,000	(25,000 × 500) – (800,000 + (25,000 × 250)) = 5,450,000	(10,000 × 500) – (800,000 + (10,000 × 250)) = 1,700,000
Do nothing	0	0	0

	Product		
Alternative	Alpha 1	Delta 4	Gamma 7
Fixed costs	£450,000	£500,000	£800,000
Variable cost per unit	£60	£150	£250
Price per unit	£200	£350	£500

(a) *Maximin.* The worst payoff for each alternative is the *lowest* number in its row of the payoff matrix. In this case the worst case scenarios are £250,000 for Alpha 1, £500,000 for Delta 4 and £1,700,000 for Gamma 7. Therefore, the firm would invest in Gamma 7, as it represents the best of the worst numbers.

(b) *Maximax.* The best payoff for each alternative is the *highest* number in its row of the payoff matrix. In this case the best case scenarios are £3,835,000 for Alpha 1, £5,500,000 for Delta 4 and £5,450,000 for Gamma 7. Therefore, the firm would invest in Delta 4, as it represents the best of the best numbers.

(c) *Laplace.* Using this rule we assign equal probability to all events – in this case 0.33. The weighted payoffs are therefore £1,933,333 for Alpha 1, £3,000,000 for Delta 4 and £3,366,666 for Gamma 7. Therefore, under this rule, the firm would invest in Gamma 7, as it represents the best of the weighted numbers.

3.3.7 Gamma 7 remains marginally better under the new weighted system, with an expected value of £2,950,000.

Expected values

- Alpha 1 = (.4 × 1,895,000) + (.2 × 250,000) + (.4 × 3,835,000) = £2,342,000

- Delta 4 = (.4 × 500,000) + (.2 × 2,500,000) + (.4 × 5,500,000) = £2,900,000

- Gamma 7 = (.4 × 2,950,000) + (.2 × 5,450,000) + (.4 × 1,700,000) = £2,950,000

3.4 Decision trees

3.4.1 Machine A = £9,344,520.23

Machine B = £9,731,045.73

3.4.2 Option A – straight to production: EMV = €49,500,000

Option B – market research: EMV = €55,025,000

Therefore, Jean-Paul should carry out further market research prior to launching the product.

3.4.3 Sofa Solution should build a large factory based on EMV criteria.

EMV (large factory) = (.6) (150,000) + (.4) (–120,000) = 42,000

EMV (medium-sized factory) = (.6) (.90,000) + (.4) (–65,000) = 28,000

EMV (small factory) = (.6) (50,000) + (.4) (–10,000) = 26,000

3.4.4 She should make the deluxe range.

EMV (deluxe) = (.5) (3,750) + (.5) (2,275) = 3,012.5

EMV (simple) = (.5) (3,600) + (.5) (2,280) = 2,940

3.5 Sequencing

3.5.1 D, C, A, B

3.5.2 (a) FIFO

Total time in process = 60 days

Total lateness = 28 days

Average time in process = 12 days

Average lateness = 5.6 days

(b) DD

Total time in process = 51 days

Total lateness = 19 days

Average time in process = 10.2 days

Average lateness = 3.8 days

(c) SOT

Total time in process = 50 days

Total lateness = 20 days

Average time in process = 10 days

Average lateness = 4 days

(d) SOT

3.5.3 (a) FIFO

Total time in process = 125 days

Total lateness = 68 days

Average time in process = 25 days

Average lateness = 13.6 days

(b) DD

Total time in process = 96 days

Total lateness = 49 days

Average time in process = 19.2 days

Average lateness = 9.8 days

(c) SOT

Total time in process = 97 days

Total lateness = 46 days

Average time in process = 19.4 days

Average lateness = 9.2 days

(d) SOT

3.5.4

Job	CR	Priority
A	$(24 - 20)/2 = 2.000$	3
B	$(28 - 20)/11 = 0.727$	1
C	$(30 - 24)/7 = 1.429$	2
D	$(38 - 20)/8 = 2.250$	4

3.5.5

Job	CR	Priority
A	0.500	2
B	1.200	3
C	0.444	1
D	1.500	4
E	3.429	5
F	5.250	6

3.5.6 C, A, B, D

3.5.7 A, E, C, F, D, B

3.5.8 B, A, D, C, E, F

Chapter 4 Optimising techniques

4.1 Optimising location

4.1.1 Alton = 267.0 Brackley = 260.0

4.1.2 Re-locate to Alton, because its *ld* score (255) is now lower than Brackely's (281).

4.1.3 Tetbury *ld* score = 2,350

4.1.4 No. Frome's *ld* score is 4,030.

4.1.5

Process pair	Trips between processes (*l*)	Current layout		Proposed layout	
		distance (*d*)	*ld*	distance (*d*)	*ld*
1,3	20	2.0	40.0	1.0	20.0
2,3	10	1.0	10.0	2.0	20.0
3,4	20	1.0	20.0	2.0	40.0
3,5	30	2.0	60.0	1.0	30.0
3,6	35	3.0	105.0	1.0	35.0
5,2	10	1.0	10.0	1.0	10.0
2,6	20	2.0	40.0	1.0	20.0
			285.0		**175.0**

4.1.6 Proposed plan $= 770$

Process pair	Trips between processes (l)	Current layout		Proposed layout	
		distance (d)	ld	distance (d)	ld
1,2	100	1	100	1	100
1,6	30	3	90	1	30
6,2	30	2	60	2	60
2,3	30	1	30	2	60
2,5	20	1	20	3	60
2,9	50	3	150	1	50
9,3	50	2	100	1	50
5,3	20	2	40	3	60
3,4	100	3	300	1	100
4,7	100	1	100	1	100
7,8	100	1	100	1	100
			1,090		**770**

4.1.7 Room 502 $ld = 765$ Room 360 $ld = 814$

4.1.8 $\bar{x} = \dfrac{(8 \times 12) + (17 \times 9) + (29 \times 17) + (42 \times 14)}{52} = 25.58$

$\bar{y} = \dfrac{(5 \times 12) + (22 \times 9) + (16 \times 17) + (30 \times 14)}{52} = 18.27$

4.1.9 $\bar{x} = 7.34$ $\bar{y} = 4.73$

4.1.10 $\bar{x} = 6.93$ $\bar{y} = 5.05$

4.1.11 (a) $\bar{x} = 3.88$ $\bar{y} = 6.69$

(b) $ld = 940.3$

4.2 Optimising inventory

4.2.1 Cycle inventory $= \dfrac{Q}{2} = \dfrac{500}{2} = 250$ toasters

Pipeline inventory $= dL = (70 \text{ toasters/week}) (2 \text{ weeks}) = 140$ toasters

Safety stock (buffer inventory) $= \dfrac{70}{7} \times 4 = 40$ toasters

Average inventory $= 250 + 140 + 40 = 430$ toasters

4.2.2 Cycle inventory $= \dfrac{Q}{2} = \dfrac{750}{2} = 375$ toasters

Pipeline inventory $= dL = (70 \text{ toasters/week}) (2 \text{ weeks}) = 140$ toasters

Safety stock (buffer inventory) $= \dfrac{70}{7} \times 10 = 100$ toasters

Average inventory $= 375 + 140 + 100 = 615$ toasters

4.2.3   Overland transportation = ((annual holding costs × product value) / 365 days)) × 5

$$= ((.25 \times 4{,}000) / 365)) \times 5 = €13.70$$

Airfreight transportation = (daily holding cost × 2) + 50.00

$$= €55.48$$

4.2.4 $Q_o = EOQ = \sqrt{\dfrac{2C_oD}{C_h}}$

$$Q_o = EOQ = \sqrt{\frac{2 \times 150 \times 25{,}000}{0.3 \times 240}} = \sqrt{\frac{7{,}500{,}000}{72}} = \sqrt{104{,}166.67}$$

$$= 322.75$$

Total cost, $C_t = \dfrac{C_hQ}{2} + \dfrac{C_oD}{Q} = \dfrac{72 \times 322.75}{2} + \dfrac{150 \times 25{,}000}{322.75}$

$$= 11{,}619 + 11{,}619 = €23{,}238$$

4.2.5   Holding costs increase from €11,619 to €18,000.

Ordering costs fall from \$11,619 to €7,500.

Total cost, $C_t = \dfrac{C_hQ}{2} + \dfrac{C_oD}{Q} = \dfrac{72 \times 500}{2} + \dfrac{150 \times 25{,}000}{500}$

$$= 18{,}000 + 7{,}500 = €25{,}500$$

4.2.6 $Q_o = EOQ = \sqrt{\dfrac{2C_oD}{C_h}}$

$$Q_o = EOQ = \sqrt{\frac{2 \times 95 \times 35{,}000}{0.35 \times 240}} = \sqrt{\frac{6{,}650{,}000}{84}} = \sqrt{79{,}166.67}$$

$$= 281.37$$

For 250 items, $C_t = \dfrac{C_hQ}{2} + \dfrac{C_oD}{Q} = \dfrac{84 \times 250}{2} + \dfrac{95 \times 35{,}000}{250}$

$$= 10{,}500 + 13{,}300 = €23{,}800$$

For 300 items, $C_t = \dfrac{C_hQ}{2} + \dfrac{C_oD}{Q} = \dfrac{84 \times 300}{2} + \dfrac{95 \times 35{,}000}{300}$

$$= 12{,}600 + 11{,}083 = €23{,}683$$

Therefore, the company should order in lots of 300 items.

4.2.7 $Q_o = EOQ = \sqrt{\dfrac{2C_oD}{C_h}}$

$Q_o = EOQ = \sqrt{\dfrac{2 \times 5 \times 350}{15}} = \sqrt{\dfrac{3,500}{15}} = \sqrt{233.33} = 15.28$

Optimum $C_t = \dfrac{C_hQ}{2} + \dfrac{C_oD}{Q} = \dfrac{15 \times 15.28}{2} + \dfrac{5 \times 350}{15.28}$

$= 114.6 + 114.6 = \$229.20$

For 25 items, $C_t = \dfrac{C_hQ}{2} + \dfrac{C_oD}{Q} = \dfrac{15 \times 25}{2} + \dfrac{5 \times 350}{25}$

$= 187.5 + 70 = \$257.50$

Therefore, the total inventory costs are increased by \$28.30 as a result of the 25-item minimum order size.

4.2.8 $Q_o = EOQ = \sqrt{\dfrac{2C_oD}{C_h}}$

$Q_o = EOQ = \sqrt{\dfrac{2 \times 4 \times 1,600}{15}} = \sqrt{\dfrac{12,800}{15}} = \sqrt{853.33} = 29.21$

4.2.9 $Q_o = EOQ = \sqrt{\dfrac{2C_oD}{C_h}}$

$Q_o = EOQ = \sqrt{\dfrac{2 \times 50 \times 6,700}{750 \times 0.15}} = \sqrt{\dfrac{670,000}{112.5}} = \sqrt{5,955.56} = 77.17$

4.2.10   For 50 items, $C_t = \dfrac{C_hQ}{2} + \dfrac{C_oD}{Q} = \dfrac{112.5 \times 50}{2} + \dfrac{50 \times 6,700}{50}$

$= 2,812.50 + 6,700 = €9,512.50$

For 100 items, $C_t = \dfrac{C_hQ}{2} + \dfrac{C_oD}{Q} = \dfrac{112.5 \times 100}{2} + \dfrac{50 \times 6,700}{100}$

$= 5,625 + 3,350 = €8,975.00$

4.2.11 $Q_o = EOQ = \sqrt{\dfrac{2C_oD}{C_h}}$

$Q_o = EOQ = \sqrt{\dfrac{2 \times 40 \times 800}{60}} = \sqrt{\dfrac{64,000}{60}} = \sqrt{1,066.67}$

$= 32.66$ tons per order

4.2.12 $Q_o = EOQ = \sqrt{\dfrac{2 \times 40 \times 800}{40}} = \sqrt{\dfrac{64,000}{40}} = \sqrt{1,600}$

$\qquad\qquad\quad = 40$ tons per order

4.2.13 $Q_o = EOQ = \sqrt{\dfrac{2 \times 40 \times 2,800}{40}} = \sqrt{\dfrac{224,000}{40}} = \sqrt{5,600}$

$\qquad\qquad\quad = 74.83$ tons per order

$C_t = \dfrac{C_h Q}{2} + \dfrac{C_o D}{Q} = \dfrac{40 \times 74.83}{2} + \dfrac{40 \times 2,800}{74.83}$

$\qquad = 1,496.6 + 1,496.6 = \$2,993.2$

4.2.14 (a) $EOQ_{\$8.00} = \sqrt{\dfrac{2C_o D}{C_h}} = \sqrt{\dfrac{2 \times 10 \times 680}{0.25 \times 8.00}} = \sqrt{\dfrac{13,600}{2}} = \sqrt{6,800}$

$\qquad\qquad\qquad\quad = 82.46$ (not feasible)

$\qquad EOQ_{\$9.00} = \sqrt{\dfrac{2C_o D}{C_h}} = \sqrt{\dfrac{2 \times 10 \times 680}{0.25 \times 9.00}} = \sqrt{\dfrac{13,600}{2.25}} = \sqrt{6,044}$

$\qquad\qquad\qquad\quad = 77.74$ (feasible)

(b) $C_{\$9.00} = \dfrac{C_h Q}{2} + \dfrac{C_o D}{Q} + PD = \dfrac{(0.25 \times 9.00)(77.74)}{2} + \dfrac{(10 \times 680)}{77.74}$

$\qquad\qquad + (9.00 \times 680) = 87.46 + 87.47 + 6,120.00 = \$6,294.9\mathsf{3}$

$\qquad C_{\$8.00} = \dfrac{C_h Q}{2} + \dfrac{C_o D}{Q} + PD = \dfrac{(0.25 \times 8.00)(100.00)}{2}$

$\qquad\qquad + \dfrac{(10 \times 680)}{100.00} + (8.00 \times 680) = 100.00 + 68.00$

$\qquad\qquad + 5,440.00 = \$5,608.00$

Therefore, total costs, including the cost of purchases, will be min-imised when games are bought in quantities of over 100.

4.2.15 $EBQ = \sqrt{\dfrac{2C_o D}{C_h(1 - (d\,/\,p))}} = \sqrt{\dfrac{2 \times 1,000 \times 400,000}{0.3(1 - (714\,/\,5,000))}}$

$\qquad\quad = \sqrt{\dfrac{800,000,000}{0.3(1 - 0.1428)}} = \sqrt{\dfrac{800,000,000}{0.2572}} = \sqrt{3,110,419,907}$

$\qquad\quad = 55,771.14$

4.2.16 $d = \dfrac{375{,}000}{28 \times 20} = 669.64 \approx 670$ per hour

$$EBQ = \sqrt{\frac{2C_oD}{C_h(1 - (d/p))}} = \sqrt{\frac{2 \times 350 \times 375{,}000}{0.3(1 - (670/5{,}000))}}$$

$$= \sqrt{\frac{262{,}500{,}000}{0.3(1 - 0.1428)}} = \sqrt{\frac{262{,}500{,}000}{0.2598}} = \sqrt{1{,}010{,}392{,}610}$$

$$= 31{,}786.67$$

4.2.17 $d = \dfrac{375{,}000}{28 \times 20} = 669.64 \approx 670$ per hour

$$EBQ = \sqrt{\frac{2C_oD}{C_h(1 - (d/p))}} = \sqrt{\frac{2 \times 300 \times 375{,}000}{0.25(1 - (670/5{,}500))}}$$

$$= \sqrt{\frac{225{,}000{,}000}{0.25(1 - 0.1218)}} = \sqrt{\frac{225{,}000{,}000}{0.2195}} = \sqrt{1{,}025{,}056{,}948}$$

$$= 32{,}016.51$$

4.2.18 (a) $d = 125$ per week

$p = 500$ per week

$$EBQ = \sqrt{\frac{2C_oD}{C_h(1 - (d/p))}} = \sqrt{\frac{2 \times 245 \times (125 \times 52)}{5(1 - (125/500))}}$$

$$= \sqrt{\frac{3{,}185{,}000}{5(1 - 0.25)}} = \sqrt{\frac{3{,}185{,}000}{3.75}} = \sqrt{849{,}333.33} = 921.59$$

(b) The production time during each cycle is

$$\frac{EBQ}{p} = \frac{921.59}{500} = 1.843 \text{ weeks}$$

(c) The average time between orders (TBO) is

$$TBO = \frac{EBQ}{D}(350 \text{ days/yr}) = \frac{921.59}{6{,}500}(350) = 49.62 \text{ days}$$

4.2.19 (a) $d = 350$ per week

$p = 700$ per week

$$EBQ = \sqrt{\frac{2C_oD}{C_h(1 - (d/p))}} = \sqrt{\frac{2 \times 95 \times (350 \times 52)}{8.75(1 - (350/700))}}$$

$$= \sqrt{\frac{3{,}458{,}000}{8.75(1 - 0.5)}} = \sqrt{\frac{3{,}458{,}000}{4.375}} = \sqrt{790{,}400} = 889.04$$

(b) The production time during each cycle is

$$\frac{EBQ}{p} = \frac{889.04}{700} = 1.27 \text{ weeks}$$

(c) The average time between orders (TBO) is

$$TBO = \frac{EBQ}{D}(350 \text{ days/yr}) = \frac{889.04}{18,200}(350) = 17.10 \text{ days}$$

4.2.20 $R = D \times L = 500 \times 4 = 2,000$

4.2.21 $R = 1,725$

4.2.22 $S = z\sigma_L = 1.65 \times 45 = 74.25$

$R_{uncertain} = (D \times L) + S = (223 \times 2) + 74.25 = 520.25$

4.2.23 $S = z\sigma_L = 1.28 \times 23 = 29.44$

$R_{uncertain} = (D \times L) + S = (67 \times 4) + 29.44 = 297.44$

Therefore, the manager should not yet place a new order.

4.2.24 $R_{uncertain} = (D \times L) + S = (75 \times 2) + (1.65 \times 30) = 199.5$

4.2.25 $R = D \times L = 15 \times 2.5 = 37.5$

4.2.26 $S = z\sigma_L = 1.28 \times 4 = 5.12$

$R_{uncertain} = (D \times L) + S = (15 \times 2.5) + 5.12 = 42.62$

4.2.27 $Q = T - IP = 12 - (3 + 5 - 0) = 4 \text{ maps}$

4.3 Linear programming

4.3.1 The minimum cost (10) is achieved when x = 3.333 and y = 1.666.

4.3.2 The value of Z has a maximum value of 25 at x = 0, and y = 5.

4.3.3 $a = 8$, $b = 3$ and $c = 11$ and the value of the objective function = 113

4.3.4 $X_1 = 5.222$ and $X_2 = 2.222$, The maximum value of the objective function is 39.444.

4.3.5 When P = 45 and Q = 6.25, the value of the objective function is maximised at 1.25.

4.2.6 3 blocks of Food A, 0 Food B.

4.3.7 *Revenue* = *R* = €16,960 at 6,400 litres of Chemical A, and 3,200 litres of Chemical B.

4.3.8 A maximum volume of 100 cubic metres is obtained by buying 8 of Box X and 3 of Box Y.

4.3.9 The maximum profit of €700 is gained by purchasing 10 Notre Dames and 8 Eiffel Towers.

4.3.10 X=10 and Y=65.52 with the value of the objective function being SEK1866.5.

4.3.11 (a) A = 81.8, B = 32.7. The value of the objective function is €408.9.

(b) Doubling the assembly time available means that the company could make an additional profit of €408.9, so this is the *maximum* amount they should be prepared to pay for the hire of the machine for doubling the assembly time.

4.4 Transportation method

4.4.1 (a) 305, (b) 305 (i.e. they both give the same initial solution)

4.4.2 (a) 880, (b) 920 (yes, the northwest-corner method gives the best initial solution, unusual, but it can happen)

4.4.3

	X	Y	Z	Supply
A			10	10
B		20	10	30
C	20			20
Demand	20	20	20	60

4.4.4

	P	Q	R	S	Supply
A				14	14
B		10			10
C	10		4	1	15
D		5	7		12
Dummy			1		
Demand	10	15	12	15	

4.4.5 1,835

CHAPTER 6

Formula review

1.1 Time series analysis

Simple moving average $(F_t) = \dfrac{A_{t-1} + A_{t-2} + A_{t-3} + A_{t-4} + \ldots + A_{t-n}}{n}$

Where n = time periods
F_t = forecast for week t
A_t = actual demand for week t

Weighted moving average (F_t)

$= \dfrac{Weight\ (A_{t-1}) + Weight\ (A_{t-2}) + Weight\ (A_{t-3}) + \ldots + Weight\ (A_{t-n})}{sum\ of\ weights}$

Exponentially smoothed forecast $(F_t) = \alpha(A_{t-1}) + (1 - \alpha)F_{t-1}$

Where A_{t-1} = previous period's actual demand
F_{t-1} = previous period's forecast demand
α = smoothing constant

Trend-adjusted exponentially smoothed forecast $(FIT_t) = F_t + T_t$

Where F_t = exponentially smoothed forecast

$\qquad = \alpha(A_{t-1}) + (1 - \alpha)(F_{t-1} + T_{t-1})$

T_t = exponentially smoothed trend

$\qquad = \beta(F_t - F_{t-1}) + (1 - \beta)T_{t-1}$

Where A_t = actual demand for period t
α = smoothing constant for the average
β = smoothing constant for the trend

Trend projection: $y^> = a + bx$

Where $y^> =$ computed value of the variable to be predicted (the *dependent variable*)

$a = y$-axis intercept
$b =$ slope of the regression line
$x =$ the independent variable

$$b = \frac{\sum xy - n\bar{x}\bar{y}}{\sum x^2 - n\left(\bar{x}^2\right)}$$

$$a = \bar{y} - b\bar{x}$$

Where $x =$ known values of the independent variables
$y =$ known values of the dependent variables
$\bar{x} =$ average of x values
$\bar{y} =$ average of the y values
$n =$ number of data points

1.2 Associative forecasting

Computed value of variable to be predicted $y^> = a + bx$

Where $a = y$-axis intercept
$b =$ slope of the regression line
$x =$ the independent variable

$$b = \frac{\sum xy - n\bar{x}\bar{y}}{\sum x^2 - n\left(\bar{x}^2\right.}$$

$$a = \bar{y} - b\bar{x}$$

Where $x =$ known values of the independent variables
$y =$ known values of the dependent variables
$\bar{x} =$ average of x values
$\bar{y} =$ average of the y values
$n =$ number of data points

1.3   Forecast error

Forecast Error **for time period** t (E_t) = *Actual value* (A_t) – *Forecast value* (F_t)

$$MAD = \frac{\sum |E_t|}{n}$$

$$MSE = \frac{\sum E_t^2}{n}$$

$$MAPE = \frac{\sum [[E_t \ / \ A_t] 100]}{n}$$

Where n = number of forecast periods

2.1   EBIT and NPV

$$Net\ present\ value\ (P) = \frac{F}{[1 + (r \ / \ 100)]^n}$$

Net present value (P) for longer periods = *FX*

Where F = future value
R = discount rate (interest rate)
X = factor from a discount table based on a given interest rate

Annuity value (S) = *RX*

Where R = amount to be received annually
X is the factor from the annuity table based on a given interest rate

2.2   Productivity and efficiency

$$Productivity = \frac{Output\ from\ the\ operation}{Input\ to\ the\ operation}$$

$$Single\text{-}factor\ productivity = \frac{Output\ from\ the\ operation}{One\ input\ to\ the\ operation}$$

$$Multi\text{-}factor\ productivity = \frac{Output\ from\ the\ operation}{All\ inputs\ to\ the\ operation}$$

$$\textit{Throughput efficiency} = \frac{\textit{Work content}}{\textit{Throughput time}}$$

$$\textit{Value-added throughput efficiency (VATE)} = \frac{\textit{Value-added work content}}{\textit{Throughput time}}$$

2.3 Capacity and requirements calculation

$$\textit{Utilisation} = \frac{\textit{Actual output}}{\textit{Design capacity}}$$

$$\textit{Efficiency} = \frac{\textit{Actual output}}{\textit{Effective capacity}}$$

$$\textit{Availability rate} = \frac{\textit{Total operating time}}{\textit{Loading time}}$$

Where *Total operating time* = Loading time – (Not worked unplanned + Set-up + Breakdown)

Loading time = Original planned operating time of a machine

$$\textit{Performance rate} = \frac{\textit{Net operating time}}{\textit{Total operating time}}$$

Where *Net operating time* = Total operating time – Speed losses

Speed losses = Idling + Slow running equipment percentage

$$\textit{Quality rate} = \frac{\textit{Valuable operating time}}{\textit{Net operating time}}$$

Valuable operating time = Net operating time – Quality losses

Overall equipment effectiveness (OEE) = $a \times p \times q$

Where a = availability rate
p = performance rate
q = quality rate

Capacity requirement for one product/service: $M = \dfrac{Dp}{N[1 - (C/100)]}$

Capacity requirement for multiple products/services:

$$M = \frac{[Dp + (D/Q)s]\,product\,1 + [Dp + (D/Q)s]\,product\,2 + \cdots + [Dp + (D/Q)s]\,product\,n}{N[1 - (C/100)]}$$

Where D = number of forecast units (customers) per annum
p = processing time in hours per unit (or customer)
N = total processing hours per annum
C = desired capacity cushion

2.4 Work measurement

Basic time (normal time)

= *(Average observed time)* × *(Performance rating factor)*

$$Standard\ time = \frac{Basic\ time}{1 - Allowance\ factor}$$

Required sample size = $n = \left(\dfrac{zs}{h\overline{x}}\right)^2$

Where h = accuracy level in percent of the job element expressed as a decimal
z = confidence level in standard deviations (e.g. 95% = 1.96)
s = standard deviation of initial sample
$\overline{x}$ = mean of initial sample

Sample size required in work sampling (n) = $\dfrac{z^2 p(1-p)}{h^2}$

Where z = confidence level in standard deviations (e.g. 95% = 1.96)
h = accuracy level required in percent
p = estimated value of sample proportion

2.5 Failure, reliability and redundancy

Failure rate as a percentage (FR%)

= $\dfrac{Number\ of\ failures}{Total\ number\ of\ products\ tested} \times 100$

Failure rate in time (FR^{time}) = $\dfrac{Number\ of\ failures}{Operating\ time}$

$$\textit{Mean time between failures (MTBF)} = \frac{1}{\textit{Number of failures}}$$

System reliability (R$_s$) $R_1 \times R_2 \times R_3 \times ... R_n$

Reliability of components R$_a$ and R$_b$ working in parallel,
$$R_{a+b} = R_a + [(R_b) \times (1 - R_a)]$$

$$\textit{Availability (A)} = \frac{MTBF}{MTBF + MTTR}$$

Where $MTBF$ = mean time between failures
$MTTR$ = mean time to repair

2.6 Statistical process control

p-chart standard deviation of distribution of 'wrongs'
$$\textit{in a sample} = \sigma_p = \sqrt{\frac{\bar{p}(1 - \bar{p})}{n}}$$

p-chart upper control limit $= \text{UCL}_p = \bar{p} + z\sigma_p$

p-chart lower control limit $= \text{LCL}_p = \bar{p} - z\sigma_p$

c-chart standard deviation of distribution of 'wrongs'
in a sample $(\sigma_c) = \sqrt{\bar{c}}$

c-chart upper control limit $\text{UCL}_c = \bar{c} + z\sigma_c$

c-chart lower control limit $\text{LCL}_c = \bar{c} - z\sigma_c$

Where $\bar{p}$ = average percentage of 'wrongs' in the population
n = sample size of *each* sample
z = number of standard deviations (most common is $z = 3$ for 99.73% limit)
$\bar{c}$ = mean number of defects per unit

$$\textit{Population mean} = \bar{\bar{X}} = \frac{\bar{X}_1 + \bar{X}_2 + ... + \bar{X}_n}{m}$$

$$\textit{Average range of samples} = \bar{R} = \frac{R_1 + R_2 + ... + R_n}{m}$$

Where $\bar{X}$ = sample mean
m = number of samples
n = sample size of *each* sample
R = sample range

Upper control limit for sample means (X) chart = UCL = $\bar{\bar{X}} + A_2 \bar{R}$

Lower control limit for sample means (X chart = LCL = $\bar{\bar{X}} - A_2 \bar{R}$

And for the range chart:

Upper control limit for range(R) chart = UCL = $D_4 \bar{R}$

Lower control limit for range (R) chart = LCL = $D_3 \bar{R}$

Process capability ratio = $C_p = \dfrac{UTL - LTL}{6s}$

Upper one-sided capability index = $C_{pu} = \dfrac{UTL - X}{3s}$

Lower one-sided capability index = $C_{pl} = \dfrac{X - LTL}{3s}$

Process capability index = $C_{pk} = \min\left(C_{pu}, C_{pl}\right)$

Where UTL = upper control limit
LTL = lower control limit
s = standard deviation of the process variability
X = the process average

2.7 Little's Law

Throughput time = *Work-in-progress* × *Cycle time*

Work-in-progress = $\dfrac{Throughput\ time}{Cycle\ time}$

Cycle time = $\dfrac{Throughput\ time}{Work\ in\ progress}$

Servers required = $\dfrac{Work\ content}{Cycle\ time}$

2.8 Queuing methods

M/M/m queue

$$u = \frac{r_a}{(r_e \times m)}$$

$$W_q = \frac{u^{\sqrt{2\,(m+1)}-1}}{m\,(1-u)}\,t_e$$

$$WIP_q = r_a \times W_q$$

M/M/1 queue

$$u = \frac{r_a}{r_e} = r_a\,t_e$$

$$W_q = \frac{u}{(1-u)}\,t_e$$

$$WIP_q = \frac{u^2}{1-u}$$

G/G/m queue

$$u = \frac{r_a}{(r_e \times m)}$$

$$W_q = \left(\frac{c_a^2 + c_e^2}{2}\right)\left(\frac{u^{\sqrt{2\,(m+1)}-1}}{m\,(1-u)}\right)t_e$$

$$WIP_q = r_a \times W_q$$

G/G/1 queue

$$u = \frac{r_a}{r_e} = r_a t_e$$

$$W_q = \left(\frac{c_a^2 + c_e^2}{2}\right)\left(\frac{u}{1-u}\right)t_e$$

$$WIP_q = r_a \times W_q$$

Where t_a = average time between arrival

r_a = arrival rate (items per unit time) $= 1/t_a$

c_a = coefficient of variation of arrival times $= \sigma_a/t_a$

σ_a = standard deviation for arrival time distribution

m = number of parallel servers at a station

t_e = mean processing time

r_e = processing rate (items per unit time) $= 1/t_e$
c_e = coefficient of variation of process time $= \sigma_e/t_e$
σ_e = standard deviation for processing time distribution
u = utilisation of station
WIP = average work in progress (number of items) in the queue
WIP_q = expected work in progress (number of times) in the queue
W_q = expected waiting time in the queue
W = expected waiting time in the system (queue time + processing time)

3.1 Break-even analysis

Break-even in units (BEP$_x$) $= \dfrac{F}{P - V}$

Break-even in revenue (BEP$_\epsilon$) $= BEP_x P$

$= \dfrac{F}{P - V} P = \dfrac{F}{(P - V) / P} = \dfrac{F}{1 - (V / P)}$

Break-even in revenue for multiple products (BEP$_\epsilon$)

$= \dfrac{F}{\sum\left[\left(1 - \dfrac{V_i}{P_i}\right) \times (W_i)\right]}$

Break-even point for alternative processes (a or b) $= \dfrac{F_a - F_b}{V_b - V_a}$

Break-even point for make (m) or buy (b) $= \dfrac{F_m - F_b}{V_b - V_m}$

Where P = price per unit after discounts
F = fixed costs
V = variable costs
W = percent of each product/service in relation to total sales
i = each product/service

Total costs (TC) = Fixed costs (F) + Variable costs (V)

Revenue (R) = Price (P) × Sales (x)

Profit = Revenue (R) – Total costs (TC)

Value of perfect information $= EV_{perfect} - EV_{imperfect}$

3.3 Decision theory

Maximin: Anticipate the 'worst' event and select the best alternative for this scenario.

Maximax: Anticipate the 'best' event and select the best alternative for this scenario.

Laplace: All events are equally likely. Probability of each event is $1/n$. The payoff of each alternative is weighted based on these probabilities.

Minimax regret: Choose the alternative with the best 'worst regret'. Calculate a table of regrets (opportunity losses). A regret is the difference between a given payoff and the best payoff in the column.

3.5 Sequencing

$$\textit{Critical Ratio (CR)} = \frac{Time\ remaining}{Workdays\ remaining} = \frac{Due\ date - Today's\ date}{Workdays\ remaining}$$

4.1 Optimising location

Euclidean distance $D_{AB} = \sqrt{(x_A - x_B)^2 + (y_A - y_B)^2}$

Rectilinear distance $D_{AB} = |x_A - x_B| + |y_A - y_B|$

Where D_{AB} = Distance between points A and B
x_A = x coordinate of point A
x_B = x coordinate of point B
y_A = y coordinate of point A
y_B = y coordinate of point B

Load-distance score (ld) $= l \times d$

Centre of gravity $\bar{x} = \dfrac{\sum x_i v_i}{\sum v_i}$ and $\bar{y} = \dfrac{\sum y_i v_i}{\sum v_i}$

Where x_i = the x coordinate of destination i
y_i = the y coordinate of destination i
v_i = the amount to be shipped to or from destination i

4.2   Optimising inventory

$$\text{Average cycle inventory} = \frac{Q + 0}{2} = \frac{Q}{2}$$

Where Q = maximum cycle inventory

Pipeline inventory = dL

Where d = average demand for an item per period
L = number of periods in the item's lead time

$$\text{Holding cost} = \text{holding cost per unit x average inventory} = C_h \times \frac{Q}{2}$$

$$\text{Ordering cost} = \text{order cost x number of orders placed} = C_o \times \frac{D}{Q}$$

$$\text{Total cost } (C_t) = \frac{C_h Q}{2} + \frac{C_o D}{Q}$$

$$\text{Economic Order Quantity (EOQ)} = \sqrt{\frac{2C_o D}{C_h}}$$

$$\text{Total cost with quantity discounting } (C_{tqd}) = \frac{C_h Q}{2} + \frac{C_o D}{Q} + PD$$

Where P = per-unit price level.

$$\text{Economic batch quantity (EBQ)} = \sqrt{\frac{2C_o D}{C_h\,(1 - (d\,/\,p))}}$$

Where D = demand
d = demand per unit of time
p = production per unit of time
C_o = cost of ordering
C_h = cost of holding

$$\text{Reorder point in certain conditions } (R_{certain}) = D \times L$$

$$\text{Reorder point in uncertain conditions } (R_{uncertain}) = (D \times L) + S$$

Where D = average daily demand
L = lead time
S = safety stock

Safety stock (S) = $z\sigma_L$

Where z = number of standard deviations from the mean to
implement the service level
σ_L = standard deviation in demand during lead-time

Under periodic review (P) system, order size (Q) = T – IP

Where T = Target inventory position

          IP = Current inventory position (*=on-hand inventory +
scheduled receipts – backorders*)

APPENDIX

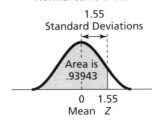

Normal curve areas

1.55
Standard Deviations

Area is
.93943

0   1.55
Mean   Z

To find the area under the normal curve, you can apply either Table A.1 or Table A.2. In Table A.1, you must know how many standard deviations that point is to the right of the mean. Then, the area under the normal curve can be read directly from the normal table. For example, the total area under the normal curve for a point that is 1.55 standard deviations to the right of the mean is .93943.

TABLE A.1

z	.00	.01	.02	.03	.04	.05	.06	.07	.08	.09
.0	.50000	.50399	.50798	.51197	.51595	.51994	.52392	.52790	.53188	.53586
.1	.53983	.54380	.54776	.55172	.55567	.55962	.56356	.56749	.57142	.57535
.2	.57926	.58317	.58706	.59095	.59483	.59871	.60257	.60642	.61026	.61409
.3	.61791	.62172	.62552	.62930	.63307	.63683	.64058	.64431	.64803	.65173
.4	.65542	.65910	.66276	.66640	.67003	.67364	.67724	.68082	.68439	.68793
.5	.69146	.69497	.69847	.70194	.70540	.70884	.71226	.71566	.71904	.72240
.6	.72575	.72907	.73237	.73536	.73891	.74215	.74537	.74857	.75175	.75490
.7	.75804	.76115	.76424	.76730	.77035	.77337	.77637	.77935	.78230	.78524
.8	.78814	.79103	.79389	.79673	.79955	.80234	.80511	.80785	.81057	.81327
.9	.81594	.81859	.82121	.82381	.82639	.82894	.83147	.83398	.83646	.83891
1.0	.84134	.84375	.84614	.84849	.85083	.85314	.85543	.85769	.85993	.86214
1.1	.86433	.86650	.86864	.87076	.87286	.87493	.87698	.87900	.88100	.88298
1.2	.88493	.88686	.88877	.89065	.89251	.89435	.89617	.89796	.89973	.90147
1.3	.90320	.90490	.90658	.90824	.90988	.91149	.91309	.91466	.91621	.91774
1.4	.91924	.92073	.92220	.92364	.92507	.92647	.92785	.92922	.93056	.93189
1.5	.93319	.93448	.93574	.93699	.93822	.93943	.94062	.94179	.94295	.94408
1.6	.94520	.94630	.94738	.94845	.94950	.95053	.95154	.95254	.95352	.95449
1.7	.95543	.95637	.95728	.95818	.95907	.95994	.96080	.96164	.96246	.96327
1.8	.96407	.96485	.96562	.96638	.96712	.96784	.96856	.96926	.96995	.97062
1.9	.97128	.97193	.97257	.97320	.97381	.97441	.97500	.97558	.97615	.97670
2.0	.97725	.97784	.97831	.97882	.97932	.97982	.98030	.98077	.98124	.98169
2.1	.98214	.98257	.98300	.98341	.98382	.98422	.98461	.98500	.98537	.98574
2.2	.98610	.98645	.98679	.98713	.98745	.98778	.98809	.98840	.98870	.98899
2.3	.98928	.98956	.98983	.99010	.99036	.99061	.99086	.99111	.99134	.99158
2.4	.99180	.99202	.99224	.99245	.99266	.99286	.99305	.99324	.99343	.99361
2.5	.99379	.99396	.99413	.99430	.99446	.99461	.99477	.99492	.99506	.99520
2.6	.99534	.99547	.99560	.99573	.99585	.99598	.99609	.99621	.99632	.99643
2.7	.99653	.99664	.99674	.99683	.99693	.99702	.99711	.99720	.99728	.99736
2.8	.99744	.99752	.99760	.99767	.99774	.99781	.99788	.99795	.99801	.99807
2.9	.99813	.99819	.99825	.99831	.99836	.99841	.99846	.99851	.99856	.99861
3.0	.99865	.99869	.99874	.99878	.99882	.99886	.99899	.99893	.99896	.99900
3.1	.99903	.99906	.99910	.99913	.99916	.99918	.99921	.99924	.99926	.99929
3.2	.99931	.99934	.99936	.99938	.99940	.99942	.99944	.99946	.99948	.99950
3.3	.99952	.99953	.99955	.99957	.99958	.99960	.99961	.99962	.99964	.99965
3.4	.99966	.99968	.99969	.99970	.99971	.99972	.99973	.99974	.99975	.99976
3.5	.99977	.99978	.99978	.99979	.99980	.99981	.99981	.99982	.99983	.99983
3.6	.99984	.99985	.99985	.99986	.99986	.99987	.99987	.99988	.99988	.99989
3.7	.99989	.99990	.99990	.99990	.99991	.99991	.99992	.99992	.99992	.99992
3.8	.99993	.99993	.99993	.99994	.99994	.99994	.99994	.99995	.99995	.99995
3.9	.99995	.99995	.99996	.99996	.99996	.99996	.99996	.99996	.99997	.99997

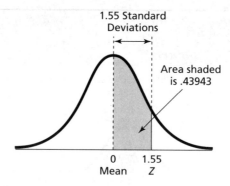

1.55 Standard Deviations

Area shaded is .43943

0   1.55
Mean   Z

As an alternative to Table A.1, the numbers in Table A.2 represent the proportion of the total area away from the mean, μ, to one side. For example, the area between the mean and a point that is 1.55 standard deviations to its right is .43943.

TABLE A.2

z	.00	.01	.02	.03	.04	.05	.06	.07	.08	.09
0.0	.00000	.00399	.00798	.01197	.01595	.01994	.02392	.02790	.03188	.03586
0.1	.03983	.04380	.04776	.05172	.05567	.05962	.06356	.06749	.07142	.07535
0.2	.07926	.08317	.08706	.09095	.09483	.09871	.10257	.10642	.11026	.11409
0.3	.11791	.12172	.12552	.12930	.13307	.13683	.14058	.14431	.14803	.15173
0.4	.15542	.15910	.16276	.16640	.17003	.17364	.17724	.18082	.18439	.18793
0.5	.19146	.19497	.19847	.20194	.20540	.20884	.21226	.21566	.21904	.2224t)
0.6	.22575	.22907	.23237	.23565	.23891	.24215	.24537	.24857	.25175	.25490
0.7	.25804	.26115	.26424	.26730	.27035	.27337	.27637	.27935	.28230	.28524
0.8	.28814	.29103	.29389	.29673	.29955	.30234	.30511	.30785	.31057	.31327
0.9	.31594	.31859	.32121	.32381	.32639	.32894	.33147	.33398	.33646	.33891
1.0	.34134	.34375	.34614	.34850	.35083	.35314	.35543	.35769	.35993	.36214
1.1	.36433	.36650	.36864	.37076	.37286	.37493	.37698	.3790t)	.38100	.38298
1.2	.38493	.38686	.38877	.39065	.39251	.39435	.39617	.39796	.39973	.40147
1.3	.40320	.40490	.40658	.40824	.40988	.41149	.41309	.41466	.41621	.41174
1.4	.41924	.42073	.42220	.42364	.42507	.42647	.42786	.42922	.43056	.43189
1.5	.43319	.43448	.43574	.43699	.43822	.43943	.44062	.44179	.44295	.44408
1.6	.44520	.44630	.44738	.44845	.44950	.45053	.45154	.45254	.45352	.45449
1.7	.45543	.45637	.45728	.45818	.45907	.45994	.46080	.46164	.46246	.46327
1.8	.46407	.46485	.46562	.46638	.46712	.46784	.46856	.46926	.46995	.47062
1.9	.47128	.47193	.47257	.47320	.47381	.47441	.47500	.47558	.47615	.47670
2.0	.47725	.47778	.47831	.47882	.47932	.47982	.48030	.48077	.48124	.48169
2.1	.48214	.48257	.48300	.48341	.48382	.48422	.48461	.48500	.48537	.48574
2.2	.48610	.48645	.48679	.48713	.48745	.48778	.48809	.48840	.48870	.48899
2.3	.48928	.48956	.48983	.49010	.49036	.49061	.49086	.49111	.49134	.49158
2.4	.49180	.49202	.49224	.49245	.49266	.49286	.49305	.49324	.49343	.49361
2.5	.49379	.49396	.49413	.49430	.49446	.49461	.49477	.49492	.49506	.49520
2.6	.49534	.49547	.49560	.49573	.49585	.49598	.49609	.49621	.49632	.49643
2.7	.49653	.49664	.49674	.49683	.49693	.49702	.49711	.49720	.49728	.49736
2.8	.49744	.49752	.49760	.49767	.49774	.49781	.49788	.49795	.49801	.49807
2.9	.49813	.49819	.49825	.49831	.49836	.49841	.19846	.49851	.49856	.49861
3.0	.49865	.49869	.49874	.49878	.49882	.49886	.49889	.49893	.49897	.49900
3.1	.49903	.49906	.49910	.49913	.49916	.49918	.49921	.49924	.49926	.49929